SCIENCE DETECTIVE A1

Higher-Order Thinking • Reading • Writing in Science

Detective products available in print, software, or eBook form.

Reading Detective® Series
Beginning • A1 • B1 • R$_X$

Math Detective® Series
Beginning • A1 • B1

Science Detective® Series
Beginning • A1

U.S. History Detective® Series
Book 1 • Book 2

World History Detective®

Written by
Deandra Dean-McLeod and Sharon Allain Smith

Graphics by
Danielle West and Brad Gates

Edited by
Erika Nelson

© 2008
THE CRITICAL THINKING CO.™
www.CriticalThinking.com
Phone: 800-458-4849 • Fax: 541-756-1758
1991 Sherman Ave., Suite 200 • North Bend • OR 97459
ISBN 978-0-89455-835-1

MIX
Paper from responsible sources
FSC® C011935

TABLE OF CONTENTS

UNIT III. EARTH SCIENCE

Introduction

The lessons in this book are designed to improve student skills in science, critical thinking, reading, and writing. The topics and skills covered are drawn from the National Science Education Standards, Grades 5-8. As an educator, you know how important it is to integrate science concepts with other subject areas. This book is an excellent tool to assist you in accomplishing this task.

The activity questions that follow each lesson require critical thinking and careful reading of text, charts, graphs, tables, and other diagrams. Students' interest will be piqued by questions with age-appropriate examples that give real-world application.

Students are frequently asked to support their answers with evidence. The evidence requires in-depth analysis of information in the text and/or diagram. This analysis helps to improve reading comprehension and critical thinking skills.

Also included is an answer key, a chart of the National Science Standards for Grades 5-8, and the numbers of the lessons covering each standard.

When to use *Science Detective*®

Science Detective® is an excellent resource to introduce or thoroughly review topics in your science curriculum. *Science Detective*® is an ideal solution for comprehensive test prep in advance of state science assessments, reading assessments, or any assessments that require students to explain and support their answers.

Grades 5-6 Science Standards

The science topics covered in this book are organized around the National Science Education Standards as listed below (for a detailed list of all science standard concepts covered by lesson, see the skills chart). Moreover, concepts and terms were derived from a survey of popular elementary science texts.

Physical Science

- Properties and Changes of Properties in Matter

- Motion and Forces

- Transfer of Energy

Life Science

- Structure and Function in Living Systems

- Reproduction and Heredity

- Regulation and Behavior

- Populations and Ecosystems

- Diversity and Adaptations of Organisms

Earth and Space Science

- Structure of Earth's System

- Earth's History

- Earth in the Solar System

All lessons contain important vocabulary and scientific terms commonly found in 5-6 grades science textbooks. Some of these terms are defined in the lesson and some must be identified through context clues.

Reading in Science

Reading in science has proven to be a challenging task requiring students to use many reading comprehension skills in order to thoroughly understand the science concepts and vocabulary being taught. *Science Detective®* teaches students to read carefully by requiring them to identify evidence that supports their answers. In fact, students must often identify information from multiple sources (text, graphs, and other diagrams) and synthesize these different pieces of information to arrive at the answer. The analysis needed to solve these problems develops critical thinking skills and greatly improves reading comprehension.

Even the **True-False Questions** involve careful analysis in this *Science Detective®* by requiring a three-step process. After reading the statement, students must review the lesson content to determine whether the statement is true or false. The students are required to give evidence by writing the number of the sentence or diagram that supports their answer. If the statement is false, students are required to replace the bold words in the statement to make it true.

Vocabulary Development is an extremely important skill in science education. Newly introduced science vocabulary is highlighted in bold text for students in each *Science Detective®* lesson. Students are required to apply these new terms when answering many of the activity questions. Other key vocabulary words that have not been defined in the lessons are used in the vocabulary activity questions, which require students to use context clues from the text to identify the meanings.

Writing

The *Science Detective®* critical thinking questions range from basic to higher-order questioning. Many questions require students to use complete sentences and explain their thinking. The ability to express their thoughts supported by evidence in writing is not only important in science assessments; it is essential when communicating with other people in school and work. It also promotes more in-depth understanding of the concepts being studied.

It is becoming more common for assessments to evaluate responses to open-ended questions in the context of logical reasoning, which has proven to be a challenging task for many students. The carefully designed questions in *Science Detective®* will develop thinking, reading, and writing skills that familiarize students with questions found on contemporary science assessments.

Suggestions

Each lesson contains one in-depth lesson page and two comprehensive question pages. It is suggested that students read the lesson page at least two times before proceeding to the question pages. The lesson page could be read aloud by the teacher or students to the whole class, in small groups, with partners, or independently.

It is highly recommended that you model the appropriate critical thinking skills for the first two or more lessons so that students understand your expectations for completing the *Science Detective®* question pages.

Follow-up Activities

To reinforce the concepts, one or more of the following activities could be done after the questions have been completed:

- **Vocabulary Reinforcement** - Have the students develop a vocabulary list with key science terms defined. By the end of the book the student would have three complete vocabulary lists: Physical Science Vocabulary, Life Science Vocabulary, and Earth and Space Science Vocabulary. Another option would be to write each vocabulary word on a notecard, with the definition on the reverse side. Encourage the students to include diagrams where applicable.

- **Share open-ended responses** - Request that the students share their answers aloud for the open-ended questions (usually #9 and #10). This gives them a chance to hear a variety of responses to the same question.

- **Correct together** - Correcting the lesson together (whole class, small group, or partners) allows the students to understand their mistakes or how answers could be improved.

- **Highlight** - Give the students a purpose to identify one or more sentences from the lesson by using their highlighter pen or by underlining. The purpose could be: most interesting, have a personal example, part they'd like to illustrate, want to learn more about, etc. Sharing these highlighted thoughts with others in the class helps to reinforce the concepts and creates motivation.

Skills Chart
National Science Education Standards[1] Grades 5-8

Physical Science	Lesson
Properties and Changes of Properties in Matter	
A substance has characteristic properties, such as density, a boiling point, and solubility, all of which are independent of the amount of the sample. A mixture of substances often can be separated into the original substances using one or more of the characteristic properties.	1, 2, 3
Substances react chemically in characteristic ways with other substances to form new substances (compounds) with different characteristic properties. In chemical reactions, the total mass is conserved. Substances often are placed in categories or groups if they react in similar ways; metals are an example of such a group.	2, 3, 4
Chemical elements do not break down during normal laboratory reactions involving such treatments as heating, exposure to electric current, or reaction with acids. There are more than 100 known elements that combine in a multitude of ways to produce compounds, which account for the living and nonliving substances that we encounter.	4, 5
Motion and Forces	
The motion of an object can be described by its position, direction of motion, and speed. That motion can be measured and represented on a graph.	6, 8, 9
An object that is not being subjected to a force will continue to move at a constant speed and in a straight line.	7
If more than one force acts on an object along a straight line, then the forces will reinforce or cancel one another, depending on their direction and magnitude. Unbalanced forces will cause changes in the speed or direction of an object's motion.	7, 9
Transfer of Energy	
Energy is a property of many substances and is associated with heat, light, electricity, mechanical motion, sound, nuclei, and the nature of a chemical. Energy is transferred in many ways.	10, 11, 12, 13, 14, 15, 16
Heat moves in predictable ways, flowing from warmer objects to cooler ones, until both reach the same temperature.	10

[1]Reprinted with permission from *The National Science Education Standards* by the National Academies of Sciences, courtesy of The National Academies Press, Washington, D. C.

Physical Science	Lesson
Light interacts with matter by transmission (including refraction), absorption, or scattering (including reflection). To see an object, light from that object — emitted by or scattered from it — must enter the eye.	11
Electrical circuits provide a means of transferring electrical energy when heat, light, sound, and chemical changes are produced.	13
In most chemical and nuclear reactions, energy is transferred into or out of a system. Heat, light, mechanical motion, or electricity might all be involved in such transfers.	2, 3, 12, 14, 15, 16
The sun is a major source of energy for changes on Earth's surface. The sun loses energy by emitting light. A tiny fraction of that light reaches Earth, transferring energy from the sun to Earth. The sun's energy arrives as light with a range of wavelengths, consisting of visible light, infrared, and ultraviolet radiation.	11, 16

Life Science

Structure and Function in Living Systems

Living systems at all levels of organization demonstrate the complimentary nature of structure and function. Important levels of organization for structure and function include cells, organs, tissues, organ systems, whole organisms, and ecosystems.	17, 29
All organisms are composed of cells — the fundamental unit of life. Most organisms are single cells; other organisms, including humans, are multicellular.	17
Cells carry on the many functions needed to sustain life. They grow and divide, thereby producing more cells. This requires that they take in nutrients, which they use to provide energy for the work that cells do and to make the materials that a cell or an organism needs.	18, 19
Disease is a breakdown in structures or functions of an organism. Some diseases are the result of intrinsic failures of the system. Others are the result of damage by infection by other organisms.	18, 22
Specialized cells perform specialized functions in multicellular organisms. Groups of specialized cells cooperate to form a tissue, such as a muscle. Different tissues are in turn grouped together to form larger functional units, called organs. Each type of cell, tissue, and organ has a distinct structure and set of functions that serve the organism as a whole.	19
The human organism has systems for digestion, respiration, reproduction, circulation, excretion, movement, control, coordination, and for protection from disease. These systems interact with one another.	23, 24, 25, 26, 27

Life Science	Lesson
Reproduction and Heredity	
Reproduction is a characteristic of all living systems; because no individual organism lives forever, reproduction is essential to the continuation of every species. Some organisms reproduce asexually. Other organisms reproduce sexually.	27, 30
In many species, including humans, females produce eggs and males produce sperm. Plants also produce sexually — the egg and sperm are produced in the flowers of flowering plants. An egg and sperm unite to begin development of a new individual. That new individual receives genetic information from its mother (via the egg) and its father (via the sperm). Sexually produced offspring are never identical to either of their parents.	27, 30
Every organism requires a set of instructions for specifying its traits. Heredity is the passage of these instructions from one generation to another.	19
Hereditary information is contained in genes, located in the chromosomes of each cell. Each gene carries a single unit of information. An inherited trait of an individual can be determined by one or by many genes, and a single gene can influence more than one trait. A human cell contains many thousands of different genes.	19
The characteristics of an organism can be described in terms of a combination of traits. Some traits are inherited and others result from interactions with the environment.	20, 21, 22
Regulation and Behavior	
All organisms must be able to obtain and use resources, grow, reproduce, and maintain stable internal conditions while living in a constantly changing external environment.	18, 33
Regulation of an organism's internal environment involves sensing the internal environment and changing physiologic activities to keep conditions within the range required to survive.	18
Behavior is one kind of response an organism can make to an internal or environmental stimulus. A behavioral response requires coordination and communication at many levels, including cells, organ systems, and whole organisms. Behavioral response is a set of actions determined in part by heredity and in part from experience.	25, 34
Most scientists believe that an organism's behavior evolves through adaptation to its environment. How a species moves, obtains food, reproduces, and responds to danger is based on this adaptation.	28, 29, 30, 31, 32, 33, 34

Life Science	Lesson

Populations and Ecosystems

A population consists of all individuals of a species that occur together at a given place and time. All populations living together and the physical factors with which they interact compose an ecosystem.	34
Populations of organisms can be categorized by the function they serve in an ecosystem. Plants and some microorganisms are producers — they make their own food. All animals, including humans, are consumers, who obtain food by eating other organisms. Decomposers, primarily bacteria and fungi, are consumers that use waste materials and dead organisms for food. Food webs identify the relationships among producers, consumers, and decomposers in an ecosystem.	28, 34
For ecosystems, the major source of energy is sunlight. Energy entering ecosystems as sunlight is transferred by producers into chemical energy through photosynthesis. That energy then passes from organism to organism in food webs.	16, 28, 29, 34
The number of organisms an ecosystem can support depends on the resources available and abiotic factors, such as quantity of light and water, range of temperatures, and soil composition. Given adequate biotic and abiotic resources and no disease or predators, populations (including humans) increase at rapid rates. Lack of resources and other factors, such as predation and climate, limit the growth of populations in specific niches in the ecosystem.	33, 34, 41

Diversity and Adaptations of Organisms

Millions of species of animals, plants, and microorganisms are alive today. Although different species might look dissimilar, the unity among organisms becomes apparent from an analysis of internal structures, the similarity of their chemical processes, and the evidence of common ancestry.	28, 31, 32
Most scientists believe biological evolution accounts for the diversity of species developed through gradual processes over many generations. Their theory is that species acquire many of their unique characteristics through biological adaptation, which involves the selection of naturally occurring variations in populations. Biological adaptations include changes in structures, behaviors, or physiology that enhance survival and reproductive success in a particular environment.	32, 33
Extinction of a species occurs when the environment changes and the adaptive characteristics of a species are insufficient to allow its survival. Most scientists believe that fossils indicate that many organisms which lived long ago are extinct. Extinction of species is common; most of the species that have lived on Earth no longer exist.	38

Earth and Space Science	Lesson
Structure of the Earth System	
The solid earth is layered with a lithosphere; a hot, convecting mantle; and a dense, metallic core.	43
Lithospheric plates on the scales of continents and oceans constantly move at rates of centimeters per year in response to movements in the mantle. Major geological events, such as earthquakes, volcanic eruptions, and mountain building, result from these plate motions.	35
Landforms are the result of a combination of constructive and destructive forces. Constructive forces include crustal deformation, volcanic eruption, and deposition of sediment, while destructive forces include weathering and erosion.	35
Some changes in the solid earth can be described as the "rock cycle." Old rocks at Earth's surface weather, forming sediments that are buried, then compacted, heated, and often recrystallized into new rock. Eventually, those new rocks may be brought to the surface by the forces that drive plate motions, and the rock cycle continues.	36, 37
Soil consists of weathered rocks and decomposed organic material from dead plants, animals, and bacteria. Soils are often found in layers, with each having a different chemical composition and texture.	39
Water, which covers the majority of Earth's surface, circulates through the crust, oceans, and atmosphere in what is known as the "water cycle." Water evaporates from Earth's surface, rises and cools as it moves to higher elevations, condenses as rain or snow, and falls to the surface where it collects in lakes, oceans, soil, and in rocks underground.	40
Water is a solvent. As it passes through the water cycle, it dissolves minerals and gases and carries them to the oceans.	3, 41
The atmosphere is a mixture of nitrogen, oxygen, and trace gases that include water vapor. The atmosphere has different properties at different elevations.	43
Clouds, formed by the condensation of water vapor, affect weather and climate.	43
Global patterns of atmospheric movement influence local weather. Oceans have a major effect on climate, because water in the oceans holds a large amount of heat.	43
Living organisms have played many roles in Earth's system, including affecting the composition of the atmosphere, producing some types of rocks, and contributing to the weathering of rocks.	36

Earth and Space Science	Lesson
Earth's History	
The geological processes we see today, including erosion, movement of lithospheric plates, and changes in atmospheric composition, are similar to those that occurred in the past. Earth's history is also influenced by occasional catastrophes, such as the impact of an asteroid or comet.	38
Most scientists believe that fossils provide important evidence of how life and environmental conditions have changed.	38
Earth in the Solar System	
Earth is the third planet from the sun in a system that includes the moon, the sun, seven other planets and their moons, and smaller objects, such as asteroids and comets. The sun, an average star, is the central and largest body in the solar system.	45
Most objects in the solar system are in regular and predictable motion. Those motions explain such phenomena as the day, the year, phases of the moon, and eclipses.	42
Gravity is the force that keeps planets in orbit around the sun and governs the rest of the motion in the solar system. Gravity alone holds us to Earth's surface and explains the phenomena of the tides.	42
The sun is the major source of energy for phenomena on Earth's surface, such as growth of plants, winds, ocean currents, and the water cycle. Seasons result from variations in the amount of the sun's energy hitting the surface, due to the tilt of Earth's rotation on its axis and the length of the day.	44

SCORING & ASSESSMENT CRITERIA

Each complete *Science Detective*® activity includes a lesson and related questions. Questions may require identification of evidence or explanations of a student's thinking. To get a good picture of a student's overall performance, we suggest using a 3-part score: 1) score answers for correctness, 2) score answers for clarity, and 3) score accuracy of evidence cited. Many teachers find the reproducible scoring rubric below to be useful in assessing student performance on these lessons.

- -

Student Name _____

Activity _____

SCIENCE DETECTIVE® SCORING RUBRIC

- Content (correct answers show understanding of concept)
- Clarity of student's explanations (complete sentences, clearly written)
- Evidence sentences and paragraphs correctly identified

Content: If the information in your answer showed complete understanding of the information in the story and graphics, you got a 3. If it showed a partial understanding, you got a 2 or a 1. If there was no evidence that you understood the information, you got a 0.

Clarity: If you communicated clearly, even if the ideas themselves were wrong, you got a 3. If your ideas were communicated poorly, you got a 2 or 1. If you were not clear and it was not possible to understand your thoughts as written, you got a 0.

Evidence: If you correctly identified all sentences or paragraphs that prove or give the best evidence for your answer, you got a 3. If you identified some of the correct evidence, you got a 2 or 1. If you did not correctly identify any of the evidence, you got a 0.

Content Score: _____ (Scale 0–3)

Clarity Score: _____ (Scale 0–3)

Evidence Score: _____ (Scale 0–3)

Comments:

_____

_____

_____

_____

To the Student

Why You Should Become a *Science Detective*®

Critical thinking, reading, and writing are as important in science as they are in the rest of your subjects. This workbook was created to improve your thinking, reading, and writing skills while you learn science.

It's All About Evidence

As a critical thinker, you need to look for *evidence* in what you read. Evidence is information that shows why something is true or could be true.

Read the six sentences below and try to answer the following question: Is the filament in a flashlight bulb a good conductor? Find the evidence that tells you the answer.

[1]The term **electric current** is used to describe the number of electrons moving through a wire every second. [2]A material that lets electrons pass through it easily is called a conductor.

[3]When electrons flow through the flashlight bulb, they pass through a thin wire called a filament. [4]The filament blocks, or *resists*, the flow of electrons. [5]As electrons are forced through the filament, they produce friction, and friction produces heat. [6]Forcing electrons through a filament produces so much heat that the wire gets white hot and *emits* light.

Information in sentence 2 tells us that a conductor lets electrons pass through easily. Sentence 4 explains that the filament does not easily allow electrons to flow through it. The evidence in these sentences together tell us that a flashlight bulb filament is not an efficient conductor.

Some questions in *Science Detective*® ask you to find the sentence(s) that give the best evidence for the answer. To help you find a particular sentence, all the sentences in the lessons are numbered and all the paragraphs are lettered. Questions may ask you to give the numbers of sentences or all the letters of paragraphs where you found answers.

You may have to go back and search the lesson for evidence to prove the answer is correct. All critical thinkers read carefully and then reread what they have read to make sure they understand what is explained. By reading carefully, they are sure that they did not miss any important information or details. It is your mission to find the best evidence for the answers to the questions. In this book, you are the detective; that is why this book is called *Science Detective*®.

Science Detective® Certificate

Awarded to

_____

for _____

Date _____

Signed _____

Unit I
PHYSICAL SCIENCE

1. Measuring Matter: Mass, Volume, and Density

A [1]Everything in our world is made up of matter. [2]Your pencil, a snowball, orange juice, and the air around you are examples of matter. [3]**Matter** is anything that has mass and takes up space. [4]The mass, weight, volume, and density of any type of matter can be measured.

B [5]The amount of matter that makes up an object is its **mass**. [6]Even though the amount of mass affects the weight of an object, mass and weight are not the same. [7]**Weight** is a measure of the pull of gravity on an object. [8]Weight changes as the pull of gravity changes. [9]If you took a book to the moon, the weight of the book would be less because on the moon the pull of gravity is less. [10]However, the mass of a book on the moon would not change, because the amount of matter would stay the same. [11]Scientists measure mass in units of grams (g). [12]A textbook has a mass of approximately 1 kilogram, which is equal to 1,000 grams.

C [13]The amount of space occupied by an object is its **volume**. [14]You can fit more dimes in your pocket than nickels, because the dimes take up less space. [15]Therefore, a nickel's volume is greater than a dime's volume. [16]Volume is measured in cubic centimeters or milliliters. [17]To measure the volume of a three-dimensional object such as a box, you first need to measure the length, width, and height of the box. [18]Use the formula in the table to review the volume of Box A and then find the volume of Box B.

V= L x W x H	Length	Width	Height	Volume
Box A	6 cm	4 cm	2 cm	48 cm³
Box B	5 cm	3 cm	2 cm	?

cm³= cubic centimeters

D [19]In addition to using the formula, scientists also use graduated cylinders to find the volume of matter in liquid form as well as some solid forms. [20]The unit for measuring volume in a graduated cylinder is a milliliter (mL), which is equal to 1 cm³. [21]Every rock has a unique, uneven shape, making it difficult to measure its length, width, and height. [22]It would be more accurate to measure the volume of the rock in a graduated cylinder. [23]Dropping the rock into a graduated cylinder partially filled with water changes the amount of matter in the cylinder. [24]The amount of water displaced is equal to the volume of the rock.

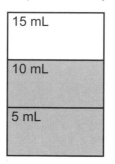 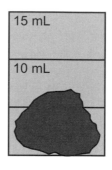

What is the volume of the rock?

E [25]You have probably observed oil floating on top of water. [26]This occurs because the water has a greater density than the oil. [27]**Density** is a measure of mass in a given volume. [28]Density can also be defined as the quality of being dense, which means to have great closeness of parts. [29]If liquids are added to the same container without mixing, they will form layers in order of density. [30]The less dense liquid will float on top of the denser liquid. [31]Even if two liquids have the same volume, the mass and density are usually different. [32]The density of an object is found by dividing the mass by the volume.

Density = mass/volume (g/cm³)

[33]Use this formula to find the density of the rock in the graduated cylinder shown above that has a mass of 30 g. [34]Did you divide 30 g by 5 cm³? [35]If so, then you found the density of the rock to be 6 g/cm³.

F [36]A substance's density stays the same even as the amount of the substance changes. [37]For example, the density of gold is 19.3 g/cm³. [38]The mass of a bar of gold could be 20 grams, 50 grams, or even 100 grams, but the density will always be 19.3 g/cm³. [39]The table below identifies the density of other types of matter.

Matter	Density
Silver	10.49 g/cm³
Water	1.00 g/cm³
Copper	8.96 g/cm³
Ethyl Alcohol	0.79 g/cm³

1. For each statement, circle T for true and F for false. If the statement is false, replace the **bold word(s)** to make the statement true. Then write the number of the sentence(s) that best supports the answer.

   a. (T) F   A brick, milk, and ice cubes are **all** examples of matter. _T_, _3_

   _____

   b. T (F) Gravity affects the **mass** of a brick. _10_

   _____

   c. T (F) As the amount of water decreases in a glass of water you are drinking, the density of the water **also decreases**. ____

   _____

   d. T (F) The volume of Box B at the end of paragraph C is **17 cm³**. ____

   _____

2. What is most likely the meaning of the word **accurate** in paragraph D?
   a. creative
   (b.) scientific
   c. careless
   d. correct

3. What is most likely the meaning of the word **displaced** in paragraph D?
   (a.) evaporating
   b. moved to new place
   c. lost
   d. contained

4. What is the volume of a rectangular container with the following measurements? (show your math)
   Height = 10 cm
   Width = 4 cm
   Length = 3 cm

   _____

   _____

5. What is the density of 500 g of juice that is 250 mL in volume?

   _____

   _____

   Write the number of the sentence that best supports the answer. ____

6. If the volume of a box is 60 cm³, then what could the dimensions be?

   Length ____

   Width ____

   Height ____

7. Complete the diagram of graduated cylinders by following these instructions.

   a. Label each cylinder measuring line by fives. Start with 5 mL and continue up to 25 mL.
   b. In the first cylinder, shade in 15 mL of water.
   c. In the second cylinder, draw a jagged rock at the bottom that has a volume of 8 cm³ and shade in the water to show the change in water level compared to the first cylinder.
   d. In the third cylinder, draw a smooth rock at the bottom that has a volume of 4 cm³ and shade in the water to show the change in water level compared to the first cylinder.

8. Find the density of the two rocks drawn in 7c, d.

   a. The jagged rock has a mass of 56 grams. This rock therefore has a density of _____ .

   b. The smooth rock has a mass of 36 grams. This rock therefore has a density of _____ .

Written Response Questions

For the following two questions, apply all of the information you have learned when answering.

9. Martha needs to figure out the volume of her rectangular bathtub. Explain to Martha the best way to accomplish this task.

_____

_____

_____

_____

_____

_____

_____

_____

_____

_____

_____

_____

10. Don would like to find the volume of his car keys. Explain to Don the best way to accomplish this task.

_____

_____

_____

_____

_____

_____

_____

_____

_____

_____

_____

2. Physical and Chemical Properties of Matter

A [1]You know now that **matter** is anything that has mass and takes up space. [2]All matter can be identified and described by its own unique set of physical and chemical properties. [3]In science, **properties** are characteristics used to identify or describe a substance.

B [4]When you look at a lemon, you know it's a lemon because of the color, shape, and smell. [5]**Physical properties** such as these can be observed or measured without changing the composition of matter. [6]You use your senses (smell, touch, sight, taste, and sometimes hearing) to observe physical properties. [7]Other examples of physical properties are: texture, density, buoyancy, luster, solubility, and conductivity.

C [8]Scientists use physical properties to identify and compare substances, such as rocks and minerals. [9]For example, diamonds are a clear, very hard crystal with a shiny luster, while talc has a very soft texture and is a whitish gray color.

D [10]Density and buoyancy are also important physical properties in identifying matter, since both relate to the closeness or concentration of parts. [11]The ability of an object to float is its **buoyancy**. [12]A substance or object with less density will float on top of a substance with greater density. [13]Pure water has a density of 1 gram per milliliter. [14]Cork floats on water, being extremely buoyant at 0.24 grams per milliliter. [15]Iron has a density of approximately 8 grams per milliliter. [16]Placed in water, do you think iron will sink or float?

E [17]The physical properties of copper make it useful for making electrical wires. [18]One of these properties includes its **conductivity**: the ability to conduct heat or electricity. [19]Another property of copper is that it is **ductile**, which means it can be heated and drawn out into a wire or thread form. [20]Glass is also ductile, and it is heated and drawn out into minute threads to form fiber optics.

F [21]Solid, liquid, or gas? [22]The form a substance takes at different temperatures is an important physical property for identifying a substance. [23]Pure water freezes at 0°C, while saltwater freezes at a lower temperature. [24]The greater the salt content in the saltwater solution, the lower the freezing point will be. [25]Water that evaporates into a gas, or is frozen into the solid form of ice, is still water in its chemical makeup, though it has very different physical properties in each form.

G [26]The ability of a substance to be dissolved in other substances is called **solubility**. [27]Salt and sugar are very soluble in water. [28]You have probably observed this when mixing sugar or salt into a liquid in the kitchen. [29]Solubility is a physical property because it does not change the chemical makeup of the substance.

H [30]**Chemical properties** describe the changes in a substance when combined with elements such as water, air, and fire. [31]**Flammability** is a substance's ability to burn. [32]You know that wood is flammable, but water is not. [33]Burning is a chemical reaction because the wood is permanently changed into ash and gases. [34]Some gases, such as hydrogen, are also flammable, having the potential to ignite and explode given the right conditions.

I [35]Metals, in general, have the chemical property of reacting with an acid. [36]Zinc reacts with hydrochloric acid to produce hydrogen gas. [37]When iron combines with oxygen, it forms rust. [38]Copper combines with oxygen to form the mineral cuprite. [39]All of these reactions are examples of chemical properties because they change the chemical makeup of the substance. [40]Study the table below to learn some properties of silver and potassium.

Metal	Physical Property	Chemical Property
Silver	very ductile and malleable	tarnishes with exposure to air containing sulfur
Potassium	silvery white	catches fire when exposed to water

1. For each statement, circle T for true and F for false. If the statement is false, replace the **bold word(s)** to make the statement true. Then write the number of the sentence(s) that best supports the answer.

   a. T F All matter has **the same** properties. _____

   _____

   b. T F Iron is not buoyant in water because it has a **greater density** than water. ____ , ____ , ____

   _____

   c. T F **Chemical properties** are reactions that change the chemical composition of a substance. ____

   _____

   d. T F Many substances become more ductile as the **temperature is increased**. ____

   _____

2. In paragraph C, the word **luster** most likely means:
   a. dullness
   b. hardness
   c. transparent
   d. shining by reflecting light

   Write the number of the sentence that best supports the answer. ____

3. Which of the following items is probably the most ductile?
   a. slice of bread
   b. piece of chewed gum
   c. wooden blocks
   d. piece of paper

4. Describe several physical properties for each of the following items.
   a. Rose

   _____

   b. Basketball

   _____

   c. Metal cooking pot

   _____

   d. Ice cube

   _____

Use the following table while answering questions 5 and 6.

Density of Substances

Substances	grams per milliliter
Gasoline	0.73
Silver	10.49
Lead	11.34
Ethyl Alcohol	0.79
Diamond	3.5

5. Which substances from the table are buoyant in pure water? Explain why.

   _____

   _____

   _____

   Write the numbers of the two sentences that best support the answer. ____, ____

6. Explain why the other substances are not buoyant in pure water.

   _____

   _____

   _____

7. Why do you think silver and gold are two of the most common metals used in making jewelry? (Be sure to describe their physical properties in your answer.)

   _____

   _____

   _____

8. Which property of silver may discourage people from buying silver jewelry?

_____

_____

_____

Written Response Questions

For the following questions, apply all of the information you have learned when answering.

9. Solubility is a physical property; therefore, a dissolved substance must be able to return to its original form. If you mixed a sugary orange drink powder into water, you could observe the solubility property. If you drank only half of this orange drink, what do you suppose would happen to the remaining liquid if it were left on a table for a few days? Explain what would happen to both the water and powder drink mix. Explain why.

_____

_____

_____

_____

_____

_____

_____

_____

_____

10. Crushed salt is commonly spread on icy/snowy roadways for safer driving. Using information in the lesson, explain why salt is most likely used.

_____

_____

_____

_____

_____

_____

_____

_____

_____

_____

3. Physical and Chemical Changes in Matter

A [1]Matter around you is changing every day. [2]An egg is changed when it is cracked open. [3]Frying an egg in a pan changes it in a different way. [4]Which of these changes is physical and which is chemical?

B [5]A **physical change** is a change in position, shape, size, or state without a new substance forming. [6]A solid form of matter can be changed physically. [7]For example, you can tear a sheet of paper, crush a pretzel, or cut a carrot into small pieces. [8]All of these changes allow the material to keep its identity.

C [9]Another physical change is when matter changes state (or phase). [10]Changing from a solid to a liquid to a gas does not change the chemical makeup of the matter. [11]Every substance changes from one state to another at different temperatures. [12]The temperature at which a substance changes from a solid to a liquid is called the **melting point**. [13]For example, the melting point of ice is 0°C, and the melting point of sugar is 185°C.

D [14]A liquid can change into either a solid or a gas. [15]**Evaporation** occurs when liquid molecules at the surface become gas molecules. [16]As the temperature of the liquid increases, the evaporation of the molecules becomes more rapid. [17]When the liquid reaches a high enough temperature, it will begin to boil, which means that liquid molecules below the surface will turn into gas molecules and then rise to the surface as bubbles. [18]This temperature is called the **boiling point**. [19]Every substance has a different boiling point. [20]For example, water boils at 100°C, and acetic acid boils at 118°C. [21]When gas particles released from the boiling process touch a cold surface, they will change back to a liquid. [22]This physical change is called **condensation**.

E [23]By mixing lemon juice, water, and sugar together, you create a mixture known as lemonade. [24]A mixture is another example of a physical change. [25]A **mixture** is a combination of substances in which the substances keep their own properties and do not bond to form a chemical compound.

F [26]One type of mixture is called a suspension. [27]A **suspension** is a mixture of particles that separate upon "standing," or remaining still for a period of time. [28]Italian salad dressing is a good example of a suspension. [29]Before pouring this dressing over your salad, you must shake it well to remix the components that have separated. [30]After shaking, you can watch the oil, vinegar, and seasonings separate again.

G [31]An instant drink made by combining a powdery substance and water is an example of another mixture, called a solution. [32]In a **solution**, one substance is dissolved in another. [33]Saltwater is also a solution. [34]Salt is soluble in water, which means it can be dissolved. [35]The salt particles are referred to as the **solute**, which means they become dissolved, and the water is called the **solvent**, because it is the part of the solution that dissolves a substance.

H [36]Cutting a loaf of bread into slices only changes the bread physically. [37]However, once a slice of bread is toasted, it has gone through a chemical change. [38]Following a **chemical change**, the substances are altered chemically and display different properties. [39]Heat, light, color change, and fizzing are commonly caused by chemical change. [40]Green leaves change to many different brilliant colors in autumn. [41]This color change is a direct result of a chemical change taking place within the leaves. [42]Two other chemical changes that you have probably observed through a change in color are rust forming on an iron object and mold growing on food.

I [43]A piece of wood burning is a chemical change known as **combustion**. [44]Burning wood releases energy in the form of heat and light produced from the fire. [45]Energy can also be absorbed in a substance as it undergoes a chemical change. [46]Baking cookies involves the absorption of energy. [47]Can you think of other chemical changes that take place due to the release or absorption of energy?

1. For each statement, circle T for true and F for false. If the statement is false, replace the **bold word(s)** to make the statement true. Then write the number of the sentence(s) that best supports the answer.
   a. T F Water droplets forming on a window on a cool day is an example of **evaporation**.

   _____, _____

   _____

   b. T F Boiling occurs when molecules **begin changing from liquid to gas**.

   _____

   _____

   c. T F A mixture **cannot be reversed** back to its original properties. _____

   _____

   d. T F All substances have **the same melting point**. _____, _____

   _____

2. In paragraph E, the word **bond** means the same as:
   a. erase
   b. melt
   c. connect
   d. change color

3. A banana ripening from green to yellow to brown is an example of:
   a. a mixture.
   b. physical change.
   c. chemical change.
   d. combustion.

   Write the numbers of the two sentences that best support the answer. _____, _____

4. Draw a diagram of a suspension. Illustrate Italian salad dressing before being mixed and when mixed.

unmixed	mixed

5. Explain how condensation and evaporation are opposites.

   _____

   _____

   _____

   Write the numbers of the two sentences that best support the answer. _____, _____

6. Complete the chart below as you identify a physical or chemical change for some common objects.

Changes		
Objects	**Physical**	**Chemical**
apple		pieces turn brown
leaf	animal bite	
egg and milk	blend together	cook into scrambled eggs
cheese		grows mold
paper bag	rips	

7. Identify the solute and solvent for each solution in the chart.

Solution	Solute	Solvent
Saltwater		
Orange Drink – made by mixing orange powder in water		
Chocolate Milk - made by mixing milk and chocolate powder together		

Written Response Questions

For the following questions, apply all of the information you have learned when answering.

8. A candle demonstrates good examples of physical and chemical changes. While the candlewick is burning, the wax is melting. Explain which of these changes is physical and which is chemical. Explain how you know.

_____

_____

_____

_____

_____

_____

_____

9. Explain step-by-step how you would make pancakes. For each step, tell if it is a physical or chemical change.

_____

_____

_____

_____

_____

_____

_____

4. Atoms, Elements, and Compounds

A [1]Gold, carbon, calcium, cobalt, and oxygen are just a few of the more than 112 elements known today. [2]**Elements** are pure substances that cannot be broken down any further without breaking the atoms themselves. [3]All matter is made up of elements, even your body. [4]Look at the circle graph below to see which elements make up your body.

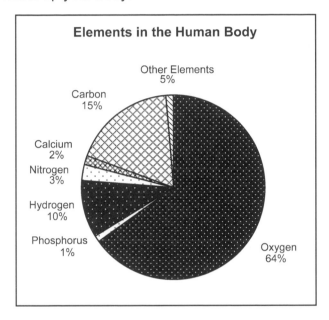

Elements in the Human Body

Other Elements 5%
Carbon 15%
Calcium 2%
Nitrogen 3%
Hydrogen 10%
Phosphorus 1%
Oxygen 64%

B [5]Elements are made up of atoms. [6]**Atoms** are among the smallest basic units of matter. [7]These units, or particles, have the same chemical properties as the element itself. [8]Atoms are made up of three **subatomic particles**: protons, which carry a positive charge; neutrons, which carry no charge; and electrons, which carry a negative charge. [9]The **protons** and **neutrons** are joined together in the central part of the atom called the **nucleus**. [10]The **electrons** circle the nucleus. [11]Atoms always have equal numbers of electrons and protons, which means they have no net charge. [12]Most atoms have at least as many neutrons as protons. [13]Identify the particles of the helium atom below.

Helium Atom

C [14]A **molecule** is the smallest physical unit of a substance that can exist independently. [15]It consists of one or more atoms joined together chemically. [16]A **compound** is a substance composed of two or more elements that are chemically combined to form a new substance. [17]Table sugar, water, and chalk are all familiar compounds. [18]The properties of compounds differ from the properties of the elements from which they are made. [19]For example, the elements sodium and chlorine combine to form the compound sodium chloride, which we refer to as table salt. [20]Chlorine is described as a greenish yellow, poisonous gas. [21]Sodium is described as a silvery, white metal. [22]However, when these two elements combine to form the compound sodium chloride, the properties become very different. [23]How would you describe the properties of this compound that you know of as table salt?

D [24]The **periodic table of elements** organizes all of the elements according to similarities in their chemical and physical properties. [25]One way the elements are organized is in order of their atomic number. [26]The **atomic number** of an element is the number of protons in the nucleus of its atom. [27]Look back at the diagram of the helium atom. [28]What is the atomic number of helium? [29]The periodic table also groups each element by its properties: metals, nonmetals, and metalloids. [30]Metals are shiny and are good conductors of heat and electricity. [31]Nonmetals are the opposite of metals. [32]Metalloids have some of the same properties as metals and some of the same properties as nonmetals. [33]Below is the metal aluminum as it would appear on the periodic table of elements. [34]The element's symbol appears in the center. [35]The number at the top is the atomic number. [36]The number below the symbol is the **atomic mass**, which is the mass of an atom at rest.

13
Al
27

1. For each statement, circle T for true and F for false. If the statement is false, replace the **bold word(s)** to make the statement true. Then write the number of the sentence(s) that best supports the answer.

    a. T F Phosphorus is a type of **element**. ____

    _____

    b. T F Elements have **different chemical properties** than their atoms. ____

    _____

    c. T F Compounds have the **same properties** as the elements they are made from.

    _____

    d. T F The atomic number for aluminum is **27**. ____

    _____

2. How many elements does the human body contain?
    a. zero
    b. four
    c. seven
    d. more than seven

3. Helium has a total of 6:
    a. protons.
    b. neutrons.
    c. electrons.
    d. protons, neutrons, and electrons.
    The helium diagram and sentence ____ best support this answer.

4. On the previous page, label the three subatomic particles on the helium atom diagram.

    Write the numbers of the 3 sentences that best support the answer. ____, ____, ____

5. Complete the following sentence that explains why atoms have no net charge.

    Atoms carry no net charge because the

    _____

carry a neutral charge and there are equal quantities of positively charged

    _____

and negatively charged

    _____

The element sodium, which is a metal, was first identified by Humphry Davy in 1807. The technical name for sodium is natrium, which is why the symbol for sodium is Na. A sodium atom contains 12 neutrons, 11 protons, and 11 electrons. Sodium has an atomic mass of 23.

6. Fill in the box below for the element sodium, showing how it would appear in the periodic table of elements.

    ┌─────────────────┐
    │   │
    │   │
    │   │
    │   │
    │   │
    └─────────────────┘

6	7	8	9	10
C	**N**	**O**	**F**	**Ne**
12	14	16	19	20

    C = carbon
    N = nitrogen
    O = oxygen
    F = fluorine
    Ne = neon

7. Above is a small section of the periodic table of elements and a key for the symbols. Answer the following questions about these elements.

    a. What is the atomic number of oxygen? _____

    b. What is the atomic mass of carbon? _____

c. How many protons does neon have? _____

d. How many electrons does neon have? _____

e. How many electrons does nitrogen have? _____

Draw and label the protons, electrons, neutrons, and nucleus of the following atoms. You will need to use information from the lesson to estimate the number of neutrons.

8. Fluorine Atom:

9. Carbon Atom:

Written Response Question

For the following question, apply all of the information you have learned when answering.

10. Describe table salt by naming many of its properties. Then explain how these properties differ from the properties of the two elements that compose salt.

_____

_____

_____

_____

_____

_____

_____

_____

_____

_____

_____

_____

_____

5. Chemicals: Helpful and Harmful

A [1]Cleaning supplies such as bleach, ammonia, detergent, and oven cleaners are used daily to keep our homes clean and sanitary. [2]However, not following the directions or mixing the cleaners can result in burns, explosions, lung damage, and even death.

> Ammonia + Bleach = Deadly Solution

B [3]How would you determine if a chemical substance is harmful or helpful? [4]Sometimes it just depends on the amount of the substance and how it is being used. [5]In certain amounts, chlorine is **toxic** (deadly). [6]When chlorine is mixed with large amounts of water, however, it keeps our swimming pool water clean and even kills germs in our drinking water.

C [7]A chemical pH test can be conducted on drinking water, pool water, or any other substance we want to study. [8]The initials **pH** stand for the scientific term "Potential of Hydrogen." [9]A **pH scale** measures the strength of acids and bases ranging from 0 to 14. [10]By simply dipping a piece of universal indicator paper into a substance, pH can be measured. [11]A chemical change will show on the indicator paper as a color change that can be matched on the pH scale.

D [12]If there is a presence of **acid** in a substance, the indicator paper will turn a reddish color. [13]Acids have a pH value less than 7. [14]Citric acid is an acid found in fruits, such as lemons, oranges, and grapefruit. [15]Acids taste sour. [16]In fact, the word *acid* comes from the Latin word *acere*, meaning sour.

E [17]If there is a presence of a **base**, also known as alkaline, the indicator paper will turn a bluish color and will have a value greater than 7 on the pH scale. [18]Substances that contain bases, such as ammonia and soap, have a bitter taste and feel slippery and soapy. [19]However, when trying to identify a substance, it is never recommended to taste, smell, or touch the substance.

F [20]The substances that indicate a pH level in the middle of the pH scale (pH=7) are called neutrals. [21]A **neutral** substance is neither acidic nor alkaline. [22]It has no chemical reaction with the indicator paper, and the color will remain unchanged. [23]Study the pH scale below to learn the pH level of many common items.

pH Color	pH	Substance
*Deep Red	0	Hydrochloric Acid
	1	Battery Acid
	2	Lemon Juice
	3	Vinegar, Orange Juice, Soft Drinks
	4	Tomatoes, Grapes
*Lighter Red	5	Boric Acid, Black Coffee
	6	Rainwater, Milk
	7	Pure Water, Human Saliva
	8	Chicken Eggs, Human Blood, Seawater
*Lighter Blue	9	Baking Soda
	10	
	11	Soap, Ammonia
	12	
	13	Bleach, Oven Cleaner
*Darker Blue	14	Lye, Sodium Hydroxide

G [24]Products at the extremes of the scale, near 14 and near 1, are very hazardous substances. [25]Scientists only handle these substances with great caution and protective devices.

*pH scale colors can vary

1. For each statement, circle T for true and F for false. If the statement is false, replace the **bold word(s)** to make the statement true. Then write the number of the sentence(s) that best supports the answer.

    a. T   F   Chemical substances are **dangerous to taste, but smelling and touching the chemicals are safe.** ____

    _____

    b. T   F   Bleach mixed with ammonia makes a **toxic combination.** ____

    _____

    c. T   F   **The higher the pH number is** on the pH scale, the more dangerous the substance is. ____

    _____

    d. T   F   Pure water is **neutral** on the pH scale. ____

    _____

2. What could you conclude if the food you are eating has a sour taste?

    a. It is a base and greater than five on the pH scale.
    b. It is a base and less than seven on the pH scale.
    c. It is an acid and greater than seven on the pH scale.
    d. It is an acid and less than seven on the pH scale.

    Write the numbers of the two sentences that best support the answer.   ____, ____

3. A mixture of one cup of lemon juice and two cups of water would probably have a pH level of:

    a. 2 or less.
    b. between 7-8.
    c. between 4-5.
    d. 9 or greater.

4. How does adding milk to a cup of coffee change the presence of acid?

    _____

    _____

    _____

5. If someone you know is very sensitive to acidic foods, which foods would you recommend he or she avoid?

    _____

    _____

    Which foods would you recommend that person eat?

    _____

    _____

6. How would you know if you were eating something with a high alkaline level?

    _____

    _____

    Write the numbers of the two sentences that best support the answer.   ____, ____

    Your skin has an "acid mantle" that protects it from infections. This mantle contains naturally produced acids and helps to keep skin pH levels between 4 and 5.5.

7.   a. If you tested your skin for pH level, what color would you most likely see on the universal indicator paper?

    _____

    Write the number of the sentence that best supports the answer.   ____

    b. Write two more facts that you have learned about the pH levels in the human body.

    _____

    _____

8. As you have learned, many chemical substances around your home can be toxic. Therefore, it is extremely important to keep these items out of the reach of young children. Label the containers on the top shelf to the right with the names of some hazardous chemicals.

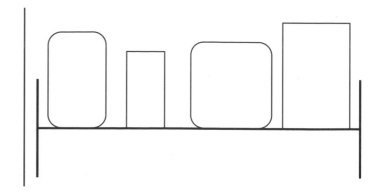

Written Response Questions

For the following two questions, apply all of the information you have learned when answering.

9. Now that you have shown which chemicals belong out of the reach of children, what would you explain to a parent who was unaware of these dangers?

_____

_____

_____

_____

_____

_____

_____

_____

_____

_____

10. Besides being harmful, many chemicals are very helpful. Explain the helpfulness of at least two chemicals.

_____

_____

_____

_____

_____

_____

_____

_____

_____

6. Kinetic and Potential Energy

A [1]**Energy** is defined as the capacity to do work. [2]There are many different forms of energy, including chemical, nuclear, and electromagnetic. [3]Energy can change from one form to another. [4]One form of energy is **kinetic energy**: the energy of a moving object. [5]A ball rolling down a hill has kinetic energy. [6]Greater speed and/or greater mass will produce greater kinetic energy. [7]For example, a tennis ball has less mass than a bowling ball. [8]Therefore, if they are both rolling at the same speed, the tennis ball does not have as much kinetic energy as a bowling ball. [9]If the tennis ball rolls at a much faster speed, however, it could have as much or even more kinetic energy than the slower bowling ball.

B [10]A ball that is set at the top of a hill but is not moving still has energy due to its position. [11]This stored energy is called **potential energy**. [12]The amount of potential energy depends on the position of the object. [13]**Gravitational potential energy** is energy gained by the height of the object above the ground. [14]Therefore, any object above the ground has gravitational potential energy. [15]For example, your potential energy is greater if you stand at the top of a high dive instead of a low diving board. [16]Once you jump off the diving board, your potential energy changes into kinetic energy because you are now a moving object. [17]Watching a pendulum swing back and forth is an easy way to observe gravitational potential energy being transferred to kinetic energy and back again.

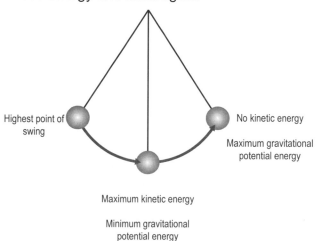

Highest point of swing

No kinetic energy

Maximum gravitational potential energy

Maximum kinetic energy

Minimum gravitational potential energy

C [18]The scientific definition of **work** is to apply a force to an object to move it through a distance. [19]You're doing work if you lift up a stack of books off of the table because you're moving them a distance. [20]Are you doing work if you stand in one place holding those books? [21]No, you're not doing work because while you are applying a force, you are not applying that force over a distance.

D [22]You can calculate the amount of work you've done by using the following formula:

$$W = F \times D$$
work = force (push or pull) X distance

[23]Force is measured in metric units called Newtons (N). [24]One **Newton** is the force needed to change the speed of a one-kilogram object by one meter per second each second. [25]Use the formula to calculate the amount of work that needs to be done to move the box below a distance of 10 meters.

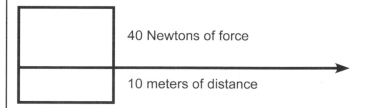

40 Newtons of force

10 meters of distance

[26]If you multiplied the force of 40 N times the distance of 10 m, the work equals 400 joules. [27]Simply stated, the amount of energy needed to move the box is 400 joules. [28]A **joule** is defined as the amount of work done by a force of 1 Newton acting through a distance of 1 meter. [29]How would the values in the formula change if you placed the box in a wagon? [30]Would you be doing as much work now to pull the box the same distance? [31]The wheels on the wagon help to decrease the force required to move the box because they reduce friction. [32]Therefore, it would be easier to do your work by pulling the box in the wagon. [33]**Friction** is a force that resists relative motion of one surface past another. [34]A baseball rolling on a rough surface, such as sand, experiences more friction than it would if it were rolled on a smooth surface, such as a wood floor.

1. For each statement, circle T for true and F for false. If the statement is false, replace the **bold word(s)** to make the statement true. Then write the number of the sentence(s) that best supports the answer.

    a. T   F   A pencil **rolling off a desk** has kinetic energy. _____

    _____

    b. T   F   A pencil **set on a desktop** has potential energy. _____, _____

    _____

    c. T   F   A very strong person who is holding a 500-pound weight off the ground **is demonstrating work**.

    _____, _____

    _____

    d. T   F   An object with greater mass **will always** have more kinetic energy than an object with less mass. _____

    _____

2. In paragraph B, what is most likely the meaning of the word **transferred**?
    a. to do work
    b. move from one place to another
    c. changed
    d. rolling motion

3. In paragraph D, what is most likely the meaning of the word **formula**?
    a. a three-dimensional shape
    b. numbers on a calculator
    c. a rule or principle usually shown in symbols
    d. a measurement

4. After reviewing the pendulum diagram, answer the following questions:
    a. When does the pendulum have the most gravitational potential energy?

    _____

    _____

    Write the numbers of the two sentences that best support the answer. _____, _____

    b. Does the pendulum have any kinetic energy at this point? Why or why not?

    _____

    _____

    _____

    Write the numbers of the two sentences that best support the answer. _____, _____

5. Kayla moved a full shopping bag using the force of 25 Newtons over a distance of 10 meters. How much energy did Kayla use to move the bag? (show the calculations)

    ┌─────────────────────────────┐
    │   │
    │   │
    │   │
    │   │
    └─────────────────────────────┘

6. Carrie moved a suitcase a total of 12 meters from her room to the front door. She used a force of 50 Newtons. What is the amount of work Carrie did to move the suitcase? (show the calculations)

    ┌─────────────────────────────┐
    │   │
    │   │
    │   │
    └─────────────────────────────┘

7. Imagine a large oak tree with many branches filled with acorns. Would the acorns on the lowest branch or the highest branch have more potential energy? Explain why.

    _____

    _____

    _____

8. A stretched rubber band has potential energy. How does the energy change once the rubber band is released? Explain.

    _____

    _____

Written Response Questions

For the following two questions, apply all of the information you have learned when answering.

9. Create an original scientific example of someone doing work. Prove that your example is work by including the amount of force and distance to show how much work was done.

_____

_____

_____

_____

_____

_____

_____

_____

_____

_____

_____

_____

_____

_____

10. Create an original scientific example of someone using force but NOT doing work.

_____

_____

_____

_____

_____

_____

_____

_____

_____

_____

_____

_____

_____

_____

_____

7. Force and Motion

A [1]You may associate Sir Isaac Newton with an apple falling from a tree. [2]His book, *Principia*, published in 1686, was about much more. [3]In this book he combined his ideas on the motion of objects with the ideas of many other scientists. [4]A **force** is a push or a pull that has size and direction. [5]The force of wind can push a piece of paper. [6]Force can be applied by your arms to pull a rope. [7]**Friction** is the force that resists the movement of one surface past another. [8]**Kinetic friction**, sometimes referred to as "sliding friction," opposes the motion of a moving body. [9]Sledding or skiing down a snowy hill is an example of kinetic friction. [10]**Static friction** opposes movement from a resting position, so there is no movement.

B [11]**Newton's first law of motion** is also known as the law of inertia. [12]The law of **inertia** states that unless a force is applied, an object in motion continues to move with a constant **velocity** (speed and direction), while a motionless object remains still. [13]A soccer ball that is sitting still will remain that way until a force of some type moves it, such as your foot kicking it. [14]The ball will continue to move until it encounters a force that changes its velocity, such as the friction against the ground or the force of hitting the soccer net. [15]Inertia is the reason you need to wear your seatbelt while riding in a car. [16]The force of a car's brakes being applied changes its velocity. [17]When the car brakes quickly, your body's inertia continues to move at the speed the car had been traveling before braking, causing you to feel like you are thrown forward.

C [18]**Newton's second law of motion** explains that force causes an object to accelerate. [19]**Acceleration** is a change in the motion of an object. [20]Acceleration of an object is related to the object's mass (amount of matter) and to the amount of force applied to the object. [21]Objects with a greater mass have less acceleration, and objects given a greater force have greater acceleration. [22]If a box of books is too heavy for you to move, you could reduce the mass by removing some of the books or increase the force by asking for someone else to help you move the box.

D [23]**Newton's third law of motion** explains action and reaction. [24]When force is applied to an object, the object exerts an equal force in the opposite direction. [25]The reaction of a basketball against the ground is one way to understand this force. [26]The basketball exerts force on the ground, and the ground exerts force on the ball.

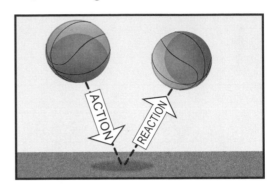

E [27]Isaac Newton also explained laws of momentum. [28]**Momentum** is the quantity that measures both the mass of an object and how fast the object is moving. [29]A large truck has more momentum than a small car that is moving at the same speed because the truck has more mass. [30]However, the car can have more momentum than the truck if the car is moving at a great enough speed.

F [31]**Gravitational force** is the force of attraction between any two objects in the universe. [32]Isaac Newton explained that the gravitational force is greater between objects with larger masses. [33]He also explained that this force increases as objects move closer to each other. [34]You can measure the gravitational force of Earth on an object by weighing it. [35]This is known as the object's **weight**. [36]Force can be measured in metric units called **Newtons (N)**. [37]One Newton is the force needed to change the speed of a one-kilogram object by one meter per second each second. [38]It takes about the force of one Newton to lift a deck of cards. [39]A **spring scale** is used to measure force. [40]The measurement of weight would decrease at places where there is less gravity, such as on the moon. [41]Study the diagram to see how a spring scale is used to measure the force of 1 kilogram.

Why do you think the unit of force is called a Newton?

© 2008 The Critical Thinking Co.™ • www.CriticalThinking.com • 800-458-4849

1. For each statement, circle T for true and F for false. If the statement is false, replace the **bold word(s)** to make the statement true. Then write the number of the sentence(s) that best supports the answer.

   a. T   F   **Pushing** a door closed is an example of force. _____

   _____

   b. T   F   The fact that a cup of water you set down will remain in that place until you or another force moves it is an example of the law of **momentum**. _____

   _____

   c. T   F   Increased force will **increase** acceleration. _____

   _____

   d. T   F   Increased mass will **increase** acceleration. _____

   _____

2. What are the two factors that affect the gravitational force between two objects?
   a. distance and speed
   b. speed and direction
   c. mass and distance
   d. mass and direction

   Write the numbers of the two sentences that best support the answer.   _____, _____

3. When a tennis ball is thrown against a wall, the ball bounces back to the person that threw it.   This an example of:
   a. Newton's first law of motion.
   b. Newton's second law of motion.
   c. Newton's third law of motion.
   d. momentum.

   Write the numbers of the two sentences that best support the answer.   _____, _____

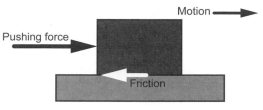

4. Which type of friction is the diagram above showing?

   _____

   Write the number of the sentence that best supports the answer.   _____

5. A baseball will move at the same speed and in the same direction until a force is applied.
   a. List three examples of what this force could be:

      _____

      _____

      _____

   b. This is an example of which law?

      _____

6. Explain Newton's third law of motion using a moving car crashing into a large tree.

   _____

   _____

   _____

   _____

7. Will a larger bike always have more momentum than a smaller bike? Why or why not?

   _____

   _____

   _____

   _____

   Write the numbers of the two sentences that best support the answer.   _____, _____

8. Review Newton's three laws of motion as you fill in the blanks within this table.

Newton's Laws of Motion	
Newton's _____ law of motion	This law explains action and _____.
Newton's _____ law of motion	This law explains that force causes objects to _____.
Newton's _____ law of motion	This is the law of _____.

Written Response Questions

For the following two questions, apply all of the information you have learned when answering.

9. Newton's laws of motion can be observed every day. Give an example of one of these laws that you have observed recently. Tell which law it is an example of and explain why.

_____

_____

_____

_____

_____

_____

_____

_____

10. A young child is frustrated because he is unable to push or pull a wagon containing two other children. Write two suggestions that you would give this child that would help with the acceleration of the wagon.

_____

_____

_____

_____

_____

_____

_____

8. Simple Machines: Inclined Plane, Lever, Machines, and Work

A [1]Some machines are extremely complex with hundreds of moving parts. [2]Other machines are simple with few or no moving parts. [3]**Machines** are devices that make it easier to do work. [4]**Work** is done when force causes an object to move. [5]Remember, work equals force (push or pull measured in Newtons) multiplied by distance: **W = F X D**. [6]Two common simple machines are the inclined plane and the lever.

B [7]Have you seen a ramp connected to the back of a work truck? [8]Ramps, which are a type of inclined plane, are used in many places. [9]An **inclined plane** is a slanted flat surface. [10]Even though an inclined plane does not have any moving parts, it makes the work of moving a heavy load from a low place to a higher place easier because less force is required. [11]However, the amount of work done is the same. [12]How can that be? [13]If the man in the diagram below lifts the load straight up, he needs to apply 300 Newtons of force upward.

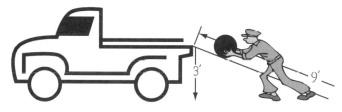

[14]If instead he pushes the load up the ramp, the man uses only 100 Newtons of force, but the distance he is moving the load is different. [15]Using the formula reviewed above, we can calculate the amount of work done as shown below. [16]Remember, a joule is the work done by a force of 1 Newton acting though a distance of 1 meter.

Lifting straight up: 300N X 3m = 900 joules of work.
Using the ramp: 100N X 9m = 900 joules of work.

C [17]A **wedge** is formed by joining together two planes. [18]On a single wedge, one of the planes is slanted and the other plane is flat, such as a doorstop (A). [19]Double wedges have two inclined planes joined to make a point, such as the head

of an ax (B).

D [20]A **screw** is a modified inclined plane. [21]The inclined plane wraps around the smooth metal rod of the screw to make a spiral. [22]Screws join parts together tightly. [23]Two pieces of wood can be held together with a screw. [24]Other items use an end that is threaded or spiraled such as a screw to hold the item in place, such as a hose or a light bulb.

E [25]A lever is a very useful simple machine. [26]A **lever** is a stiff bar that rests on a pivot point called a **fulcrum**. [27]A lever is used to help lift or move a load by applying force or effort to the bar. [28]A common example of a lever is a seesaw. [29]The board that both people sit on is the bar, which rests on a center point, or fulcrum. [30]The two people on either end take turns using their force to come down so that the other person is lifted as the load. [31]There are three different classes of levers differentiated by the order of the three parts.

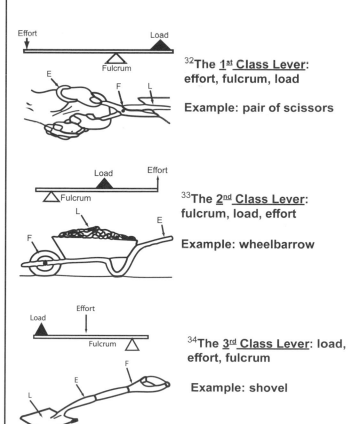

[32]The <u>1st</u> <u>Class Lever</u>: effort, fulcrum, load

Example: pair of scissors

[33]The <u>2nd</u> <u>Class Lever</u>: fulcrum, load, effort

Example: wheelbarrow

[34]The <u>3rd</u> <u>Class Lever</u>: load, effort, fulcrum

Example: shovel

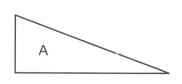

1. For each statement, circle T for true and F for false. If the statement is false, replace the **bold word(s)** to make the statement true. Then write the number of the sentence(s) that best supports the answer.

   a. T F Inclined planes and levers are machines that are **likely to be in many places** around your home. _____

   _____

   b. T F **Force or effort is always needed** when using a lever. _____

   _____

   c. T F **All levers** have a fulcrum in the same place. _____

   _____

   d. T F You **do less work** using a ramp than lifting the load. _____

   _____

2. In paragraph D, the word **modified** most likely means:
   a. partially changed
   b. separated
   c. overlapped
   d. slant increased

3. In paragraph E, the word **classes** most likely means:
   a. groups of children at school
   b. periods of time
   c. shaped
   d. groups arranged according to characteristics

4. Find the amount of work each person has done.
   a. Avery lifted a heavy box 4 meters into a truck by applying 500 Newtons of force upward.

   _____

   b. Zoe pushed a heavy box up a 10-meter ramp using only 200 Newtons of force.

   _____

   c. Who did more work?

   _____

   d. Why is it easier to use a ramp to move a heavy load instead of lifting it to a higher place?

   _____

   _____

   Write the number of the sentence that best supports the answer for d. _____

5. Name a wedge that you have seen recently.

   _____

   Draw a diagram of this wedge and then tell whether it is a single or double wedge.

   ```
   [                                ]
   [          '                     ]
   [                                ]
   [                                ]
   [                                ]
   ```

6. To which class of levers does a seesaw belong?

   _____

   Write the numbers of the two sentences that best support the answer.
   _____ , _____

7. Draw a diagram of a seesaw in the box below. Label the **force**, **load**, and **fulcrum** of this lever.

   ```
   [                                ]
   [                                ]
   [                                ]
   [                                ]
   [                                ]
   ```

8. When you twist open the cap of a soft drink bottle or water bottle, you are using a simple machine.

    a. What type of simple machine is it?

_____

b. Prove the answer: Show that it is this type of simple machine by drawing and labeling the important parts in a diagram.

Written Response Questions

For the following two questions, apply all of the information you have learned when answering.

9. What type of inclined plane have you used recently? Describe how it was useful.

_____

_____

_____

_____

_____

_____

_____

_____

10. What type of lever have you used recently? Make sure to include its lever class. Describe how this lever works.

_____

_____

_____

_____

_____

_____

_____

_____

9. Simple Machines: Wheel-and-Axle and Pulley

A [1]The wheel-and-axle and the pulley are two simple machines that make work easier. [2]Many complex machines are derived from these two simple machines.

B [3]A Ferris wheel, car tires, and bike wheels are just a few of the many wheel-and-axles we often use. [4]The **wheel-and-axle** consists of a larger wheel joined with a smaller wheel or solid shaft, know as the axle, in its center. [5]The wheel-and-axle acts as a lever rotating around a **fulcrum** (center point). [6]Effort force is usually applied to the large wheel to turn the axle. [7]In some cases, such as a ceiling fan, the rod, which is the axle, is forced to turn, which causes the fan blades, which are the wheel, to rotate. [8]Observe the locations of the wheel, axle, and

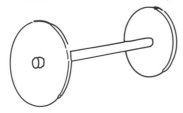

fulcrum in the graphic of the simple wheel-and-axle above.

C [9]A wheel-and-axle that has a rope or chain that fits into a groove on the wheel is called a **pulley**. [10]Where have you seen or used a pulley? [11]A pulley is used to open and close window blinds and curtains. [12]A pulley is used to raise and lower a flag on a flagpole or a sail on a sailboat.

D [13]The most basic type of pulley, known as a **fixed pulley**, makes work easier because instead of lifting up and working against gravity, you pull down. [14]As you can see in the diagram, the fixed pulley is attached to a base.

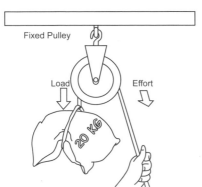

Fixed Pulley

Load   Effort

E [15]Look carefully at this next type of pulley. [16]How is it different from the fixed pulley? [17]Instead of being attached at a base, the **movable pulley** is attached to an object and moves with it. [18]Also, notice in the diagram that the movable pulley does not change the direction of the effort like the fixed pulley. [19]However, the advantage of the movable pulley is that you only use half the effort force compared to the fixed pulley. [20]The decrease in required force is due to the load of the movable pulley being lifted by two segments of rope instead of just one.

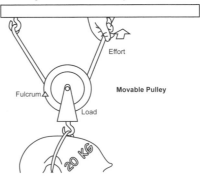

Effort

Fulcrum△   Movable Pulley

Load

20 KG

F [21]A **compound pulley**, also known as a complex pulley system, is a combination of fixed and movable pulleys. [22]The compound pulley pictured here uses the same amount of effort force as the movable pulley, but it also has the advantage of the fixed pulley, which is the change in direction of the effort force.

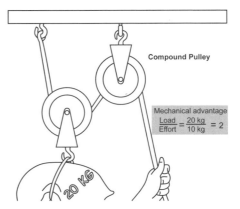

Compound Pulley

Mechanical advantage
$\frac{Load}{Effort} = \frac{20\ kg}{10\ kg} = 2$

20 KG

G [23]The amount a machine multiplies our effort is called the **mechanical advantage**. [24]To find the mechanical advantage, the load is divided by the effort. [25]The mechanical advantage of the compound pulley is 2. [26]As the mechanical advantage increases, we use less effort force to lift the heavy load, but we increase the distance we have to pull in order to move the load the same amount.

1. For each statement, circle T for true and F for false. If the statement is false, replace the **bold word(s)** to make the statement true. Then write the number of the sentence(s) that best supports the answer.
   a. T F On a pulley, load and effort **always pull in same direction**. ____

   _____

   b. T F When using a fixed pulley, you **pull down and work with gravity**. ____

   _____

   c. T F Intricate machines **have been invented** that contain wheel-and-axles and/or pulleys. ____

   _____

   d. T F The compound pulley contains **two fixed pulleys**. ____

   _____

2. Which type of pulley has a wheel-and-axle?
   a. fixed pulley
   b. movable pulley
   c. compound pulley
   d. all three pulleys

   Write the number of the sentence that best supports the answer. ____

3. In paragraph E, what is an <u>antonym</u> for the word **segment**?
   a. part
   b. section
   c. whole
   d. portion

4. Apply what you have learned from the graphics and lesson to compare in what way the movable pulley is more helpful than the fixed pulley.

   _____

   _____

   Write the number of the sentence that best supports the answer. ____

5. In what way is the fixed pulley more helpful than the movable pulley?

   _____

   Write the number of the sentence that best supports the answer. ____

   > George W. G. Ferris designed the Ferris wheel, shown below, for the 1893 World's Fair in Indiana. This huge mechanical wheel is an example of a wheel-and-axle.

6. Label the three main parts on this wheel-and-axle.

   Prove that a doorknob is also an example of a wheel-and-axle by drawing and labeling a doorknob.

7. Pulleys increase mechanical advantage, which reduces the effort needed to lift a load. Explain what else changes due to the mechanical advantage of using a pulley.

   _____

   _____

   Write the number of the sentence that best supports the answer. ____

8. Complete the table below by finding the mechanical advantage of three different compound pulleys.

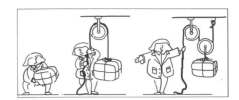

Compound Pulley	Load	Effort	Mechanical Advantage
A	32 kg	8 kg	
B	36 kg	12 kg	
C	72 kg	9 kg	

Written Response Questions

For the following two questions, apply all of the information you have learned when answering.

9. Compare and describe the first pulley and the second pulley in the picture above.

_____

_____

_____

_____

_____

_____

_____

_____

_____

10. Compare the amount of effort being used in the three different examples pictured above.

_____

_____

_____

_____

_____

_____

_____

_____

_____

10. Thermal Energy

A [1]Holding a solid chocolate chip in your hand would eventually cause it to melt because your hand has more thermal energy than the chocolate chip. [2]**Thermal energy** is the total kinetic energy (energy due to motion) and potential energy (stored energy due to position) of particles in matter. [3]The particles in the chocolate chip do not appear to be moving, but the particles in all matter are always moving. [4]The particles in a solid are pushing and pulling, or vibrating, even though they cannot move from their fixed position. [5]When thermal energy flows from one substance, such as your hand, to another, such as the chocolate chip, it is called **heat**. [6]Heat energy always flows from the hotter substance to the cooler substance. [7]The particles in the hotter substance are moving faster than the particles in the cooler substance. [8]The faster-moving particles in your hand cause the particles in the chocolate to move faster. [9]Once the particles in the chocolate are moving fast enough, they begin to flow around each other as a liquid. [10]You now have melted chocolate.

B [11]Matter can also change from a liquid to a gas due to thermal energy. [12]As the temperature of a liquid such as water increases, the particles speed up and begin to move freely as gas particles. [13]Temperature and thermal energy are not the same. [14]**Temperature** is a measure of the average kinetic energy of particles in an object, while thermal energy is the total amount of kinetic and potential energy of the object. [15]For example, if two bowls of hot soup have the same temperature, but one bowl is large and one is small, the thermal energy is greater in the large bowl of soup because thermal energy increases as the amount of the substance increases.

C [16]**Conduction** is the transfer of heat from the contact of two objects. [17]This is the only way for a solid to transfer energy. [18]In the diagram, conduction is shown as the heat from the fire transferring to the metal rod. [19]The particles in the metal rod are not changing their location, but the high temperature of the fire is causing the particles to vibrate faster and bump against other particles, which continues all the way to the opposite end of the metal rod.

D [20]**Convection** is the transfer of heat in a fluid, which can be a liquid or a gas. [21]In the diagram, the warmer air above the fire carries heat upward because it is less dense than the cooler air. [22]When the warm air rises, the cooler air flows in to fill the vacated space. [23]This cooler air is then warmed and rises upward. [24]This circular current is what we feel as wind and is called

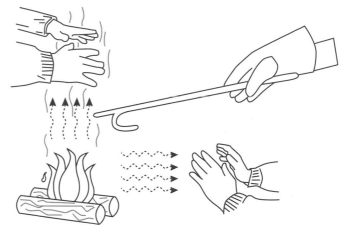

convection current.

E [25]**Radiation** is the transfer of thermal energy by electromagnetic waves. [26]Fire, the sun, and other objects give off different electromagnetic waves depending on the object's temperature. [27]Radiation can cause a chemical change to the molecules of materials. [28]The radiation of the heated coils in a toaster can cause the toast to burn. [29]The radiation from the sun can cause our skin to burn.

F [30]Sometimes you might want to keep heat contained in or blocked out of something. [31]An **insulator** prevents heat from transferring from one object to another. [32]Winter clothing insulates your body heat and keeps cold air away from your body. [33]A thermos and a cooler are made of materials that are good insulators. [34]Other materials are good conductors. [35]**Conductors** transfer heat easily. [36]A metal spoon in a cup of hot chocolate will conduct heat throughout the spoon quickly because the atoms in the metal spoon vibrate easily. [37]Skillets, used for cooking, are made of metal, such as iron, which is an excellent conductor. [38]It is smart to use an insulator, such as a potholder, when touching the skillet handle so that you do not burn your hand.

1. For each statement, circle T for true and F for false. If the statement is false, replace the **bold word(s)** to make the statement true. Then write the number of the sentence(s) that best supports the answer.

   a. T F   A jacket is an example of a **conductor**. _____

   _____

   b. T F   Solid particles **remain completely still**. _____

   _____

   c. T F   **Conduction, convection, and radiation** are three ways for heat energy to transfer from one substance to another. _____, _____, _____

   _____

   d. T F   Solid, liquid, and gas particles **move differently**. _____, _____, _____

   _____

2. In paragraph A, the word **fixed** most likely means:
   a. repaired
   b. firm and not readily movable
   c. flexible
   d. improved

3. In paragraph D, what is an <u>antonym</u> for the word **vacated**?
   a. occupied
   b. emptied
   c. traveled
   d. deserted

4. Study the diagram below. Is the temperature and thermal energy in the first container equal to (=), greater than (>), or less than (<) that in the other container? Write the correct symbol in each circle.

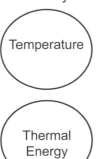

Write the numbers of the two sentences that best support the answer. _____, _____

5. Which gas particles have a greater density: hot, warm, or cool?

   _____

   Write the number of the sentence that best supports the answer. _____

6. Cake batter heats, rises, and becomes a cake after baking in the oven for 30 minutes. What type of heat energy transfer is this an example of?

   _____

   Explain why:

   _____
   _____
   _____

7. Scott scoops hot oatmeal into his bowl. He then notices that the outside of his bowl is very hot to the touch. What type of heat energy transfer is this an example of?

   _____

   Explain why:

   _____
   _____

8. While walking along the shore of a lake, Travis felt a cool breeze. What type of heat energy transfer is this an example of?

   _____

   Explain why:

   _____
   _____
   _____

Written Response Questions

For the following two questions, apply all of the information you have learned when answering.

9. Pretend you are packing for a camping trip. The weather forecast is calling for cold weather. What types of insulators and conductors will you pack? Give at least two examples of each and explain how you know they are insulators or conductors.

_____

_____

_____

_____

_____

_____

_____

_____

_____

_____

10. Lighting the wick of a candle causes the wax to melt slowly. Explain how the particles in the wax change as it begins to melt.

_____

_____

_____

_____

_____

_____

_____

_____

_____

_____

_____

11. Sound and Light Energy

A [1]Where have you seen waves? [2]When you watch a friend jump into a pool, you will see waves spread across the pool starting at the point where your friend landed in the water. [3]The force of a person jumping into the water causes water molecules to vibrate. [4]Light and sound are two more ways that waves carry energy.

B [5]Sound waves travel through gases, liquids, and solids but cannot travel through empty space. [6]**Sound waves** are caused by vibrations. [7]By knocking on a door, you are forcing the molecules in the door and the air next to it to vibrate. [8]These vibrations cause the next particles to vibrate. [9]Once these vibrations spread through the gases in the air and reach your ear, you hear the sound of the knock. [10]The measure of how fast the particles are vibrating is known as **frequency**. [11]Frequency is the number of sound waves per second. [12]Fast vibrations have a high frequency and a high-pitched sound.

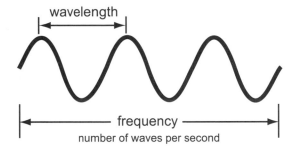

wavelength

frequency
number of waves per second

C [13]Unlike sound waves, light waves can travel through empty space because they are not a vibration of particles. [14]Light is a form of **electromagnetic wave**, which has both an electric and a magnetic effect. [15]These electromagnetic waves are sometimes referred to as radiation, or rays. [16]There is nothing that can travel through space as fast as light waves. [17]Light travels about one million times faster than sound. [18]You may have observed this during a storm when you've seen a lightning strike before you hear the thunder.

D [19]Light energy can change to heat energy when it hits matter. [20]**Opaque** materials, such as most clothing, wood, concrete, and metals, absorb light. [21]These materials do not allow any light to pass through, and some of the light is absorbed into the matter. [22]Darker colors

will absorb more light and therefore heat up more than lighter colors. [23]This is why it is a good idea to wear light colors on hot, sunny days. [24]**Translucent** materials, such as tissue paper and sheer clothing, allow some light to pass through while some light is absorbed. [25]**Transparent** materials, such as glass and water, allow almost all of the light to pass through without being absorbed.

E [26]When light does not absorb or pass through matter, it is reflected. [27]**Reflection** is when light bounces off of a surface. [28]The smoother the surface, the more likely you are to see a reflection. [29]Mirrors, smooth metal, and dishes are good examples of matter that reflect light easily. [30]When you look into a mirror, the light from the room strikes the mirror and then reflects back, so you can see yourself. [31]Since dark colors absorb more light than light colors, it follows that light colors reflect more light than dark colors. [32]To observe this theory, go into a dimly lit room. [33]Take notice of which items in the room are easiest to see. [34]What do you expect to observe? [35]Reflection and absorption are also why we see colors. [36]A blue book appears blue because it is absorbing all of the other colors except blue; blue light reflects back to your eyes.

F [37]Have you ever observed the way a straight drinking straw appears to be bent in a glass of water? [38]The light is changing speed as it moves from one material (air) to another (water). [39]This change in speed causes the light to change direction. [40]This bending of light is known as **refraction**. [41]Refraction can also occur with other materials, like glass. [42]Notice in the diagram below how the light waves bend, or change direction, when they hit the glass.

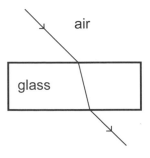

air

glass

1. For each statement, circle T for true and F for false. If the statement is false, replace the **bold word(s)** to make the statement true. Then write the number of the sentence(s) that best supports the answer.

   a. T F   A black hat is made of matter that **absorbs light energy and changes it into heat energy**.

   ____ , ____

   _____

   b. T F   Sound and light travel **at the same speed**. ____

   _____

   c. T F   **Both sound and light waves** are a vibration of particles. ____

   _____

   d. T F   **A rough surface** is unlikely to reflect light. ____

   _____

2. Seeing lightning before you hear the thunder during a storm proves:

   a. that light travels about one million times faster than sound.
   b. that there is nothing that can travel through space as fast as light waves.
   c. that light travels faster than sound.
   d. all of the above.

3. In what type of material is light refraction most common?

   a. opaque
   b. translucent
   c. transparent
   d. dark

4. For each item below, write whether it is opaque, translucent, or transparent.

   a. plastic wrap   _____

   b. wax paper   _____

   c. wedding veil   _____

   d. thick rug   _____

   e. textbook   _____

   f. window   _____

Write the numbers of the three sentences that best support the answers.

____ , ____ , ____

5. What can you conclude about slow vibrations?

   _____

   _____

   _____

Write the numbers of the two sentences that best support the answer. ____ , ____

6. Referring back to the question in paragraph E, what would you expect to see best in a dimly lit room? Explain why.

   _____

   _____

   _____

Write the number of the sentence that best supports the answer. ____

Light travels through glass at a slower speed than through air because glass is denser than air. This causes the light to refract. White light is refracted when it passes through a prism. Each color in the light is refracted at a different angle. The shorter wavelengths, such as blue, bend more than the longer wavelengths, such as red.

7. Complete the diagram below by first labeling the triangle as the prism and the line going into the prism as the white light. Then add other details to the diagram to show what you understand about how a prism refracts light.

8. What are the two most interesting facts you have learned from this lesson about sound energy and/or light energy?

    _____

    _____

Explain why you chose each fact.

_____

_____

_____

_____

Written Response Questions

For the following two questions, apply all of the information you have learned when answering.

9. While Monica was in the family room, she heard her sister, Sarah, close a cabinet in the kitchen. Explain why Monica heard this sound.

    _____

    _____

    _____

    _____

    _____

    _____

    _____

    _____

    _____

    _____

10. When you look at a green leaf, why do you see the color green?

    _____

    _____

    _____

    _____

    _____

    _____

    _____

    _____

    _____

    _____

    _____

12. Static Electricity

A [1]From toasters to computers, electricity supplies power to so many things that we use every day. [2]Sometimes we observe a type of electricity that causes clean, dry articles of clothing to cling together. [3]Electricity can be classified into two categories: current electricity and static electricity. [4]But what is electricity?

B [5]Remember, all elements are made up of tiny particles called **atoms**. [6]The three basic particles of an atom are **protons**, which carry a positive charge; **electrons**, which carry a negative charge; and **neutrons**, which carry no charge. [7]Atoms usually have equal numbers of electrons and protons, which causes the atom to carry a neutral charge. [8]However, atoms can lose and gain electrons, which changes the charge of the atom. [9]This movement of electrons causes the form of energy called **electricity**.

C [10]An **electric current** is produced when electrons are released from atoms and begin to flow. [11]Sometimes there is not a pathway for a flow of electrical charges, so the charge builds up. [12]This is known as **static electricity**. [13]You have most likely observed the shocking feeling of released static electricity while sliding on a nylon car seat or a plastic slide. [14]Perhaps you have noticed a sock clinging to a shirt as you removed them from the dryer or how strands of your hair stand up after you brush it. [15]The reason this static electricity developed is because two materials touched, causing some electrons to move from one material to the other, creating a buildup of electrons. [16]Observe in the diagram below how your hair can react when a static charge is generated. [17]Notice how two like charges push away from each other and two opposite charges are pulled together.

Static Charge

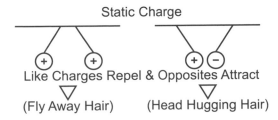

Like Charges Repel & Opposites Attract

(Fly Away Hair)   (Head Hugging Hair)

D [18]Your body is a good **conductor** of electricity, meaning electrons move through your body easily.

[19]As you walk across a carpeted floor, your feet are rubbing electrons off the floor. [20]Therefore, your whole body is now negatively charged. [21]As you reach out with your hand to touch a metal object or another person, the negative electrons jump off you and onto the other object as a spark. [22]However, if the object you touch is an insulator, such as a plaster wall or a glass, then you would transfer very little or no static charge. [23]An **insulator** does not allow electrons to move easily. [24]Since these objects resist the flow of electricity, they are also known as **resistors**.

Conductors	Insulators
Copper and other metals	Plastic
Graphite	Rope
Salt and saltwater	Wood

[25]The atoms of the conductors have electrons that are not tightly bound. [26]The opposite is true of the insulators.

E [27]**Lightning** is also produced by static electricity but with much more energy. [28]A combination of water and ice particles helps to charge the cloud. [29]The ice particles pull the electrons off the water droplets, causing the ice to have a negative charge on the lower area of the cloud. [30]The ground below becomes positively charged. [31]Since opposite charges attract, when the charge grows large enough electrons travel from the cloud to the ground in the form of a lightning bolt. [32]Observe this process below.

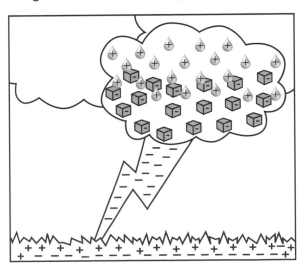

1. For each statement, circle T for true and F for false. If the statement is false, replace the **bold word(s)** to make the statement true. Then write the number of the sentence(s) that best supports the answer.

    a. T F   A lightning bolt is **negatively charged**. _____

    _____

    b. T F   A metal pole is a conductor because it allows **electrons to travel through it easily**. _____

    _____

    c. T F   Protons are attracted to **other protons**. _____

    _____

    d. T F   **A pathway is always required** for an electric current to flow. _____

    _____

2. Materials that are made of tightly bound atoms are known as:
    a. conductors.
    b. insulators.
    c. resistors.
    d. both insulators and resistors.

    Write the numbers of the two sentences that best support the answer. _____, _____

3. When static electricity is released, what moves from one object to another?
    a. neutrons
    b. protons
    c. electrons
    d. all the above

    Write the number of the sentence that best supports the answer. _____

4. What causes a lightning bolt to strike the ground?

    _____

    _____

    _____

5. Referring to the diagram in paragraph C, explain why the first part of the diagram is labeled as "Fly Away Hair."

    _____

    _____

    _____

    _____

6. Referring to the diagram in paragraph C, explain why the second part of the diagram is labeled as "Head Hugging Hair."

    _____

    _____

    _____

    _____

7. It is dangerous to be in a pool, lake, or ocean during a lightning storm. One reason is because water is a good conductor of electricity. Some other common ways for people to be injured by lightning strikes are listed here. Explain why you think these are common places for lightning strikes.

    a. Standing in open field:

    _____

    _____

    _____

    b. Golfers on golf course:

    _____

    _____

    _____

    c. Person driving tractor:

    _____

    _____

    _____

Written Response Questions

For the following two questions, apply all of the information you have learned when answering.

8. Olivia walked over to her brother, Grant, and touched him on the shoulder. Grant felt a slight shocking feeling of a spark when Olivia touched him, but when Grant touched Olivia on the shoulder, she did not feel a spark. Explain why Grant received a shock, but Olivia did not.

_____

_____

_____

_____

_____

_____

_____

_____

_____

_____

_____

_____

_____

9. Draw a diagram of this "shocking situation" from number eight. In your drawing, include a spark between Olivia's hand and Grant's shoulder. Include positive (+) and negative (-) charges within the diagram.

13. Circuits

A [1]How many electronic devices have you used today? [2]Some of them may include the TV, toaster, lamps, and computer. [3]Now try to envision what the inner electrical parts of these devices look like and how they work. [4]As you've learned, **electricity** is the movement of electrons. [5]Also, recall that like charges repel each other. [6]The negatively charged electrons repelling effect pushes electrons from one atom to the next. [7]This flow of electric charge is known as **electric current**.

B [8]Now let's picture how this current works in an electronic device. [9]The electric current must travel in a complete path, known as a **circuit**, back to its starting point. [10]A basic looped path or **simple circuit** must have a source of energy and a conductor. [11]We use **circuit diagrams** with symbols to represent the components in the circuit.

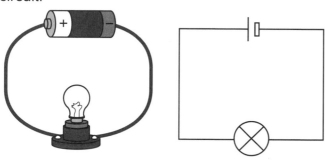

[12]Observe this circuit diagram to the right of the picture of a simple circuit. [13]Notice the symbols used for the battery (**source of energy**), the wires (**conductors**), and the light bulb (**resistor**). [14]The resistor can transform electronic energy into other forms of energy, such as heat, sound, or the light energy shown here.

switch symbol

[15]Most circuits have a **switch** to break the circuit and stop the electric current when needed. [16]If a switch is added to the circuit path, then opening the circuit can stop the electricity. [17]Closing the gap completes the circuit again and allows the electricity to flow.

C [18]Just like the simple circuit, a **series circuit** has only one path that passes through all of the components without any branches. [19]In contrast,

the series circuit path will pass through more than one resistor. [20]If a building was wired with a series circuit, then every electronic device would be either off or on at the same time.

D [21]All buildings, such as our homes, are wired with more complex circuits known as **parallel circuits**. [22]This is because a parallel circuit lets the current flow along more than one path. [23]Thus, if one light goes out in our home, the current still has other branches in which electricity can flow, keeping other electronic devices on.

Parallel Circuit

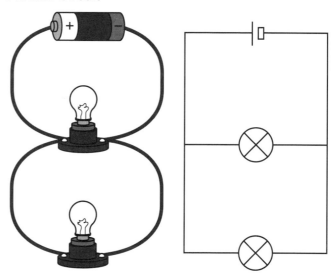

E [24]There are three measurements of electric circuits. [25]The current is measured in **amperes** (amps). [26]The resistance of the circuit is measured in **ohms**. [27]The voltage from the energy source is measured in **volts**.

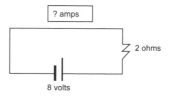

? amps
2 ohms
8 volts

[28]To find the amount of current in the circuit diagram above, use this formula:
Volt ÷ Ohms = Amps
8 Volts ÷ 2 Ohms = 4 Amps

[29]To find the amount of resistance or voltage, use the following formulas:
Volts ÷ Amps = Ohms
Amps x Ohms = Volts

1. For each statement, circle T for true and F for false. If the statement is false, replace the **bold word(s)** to make the statement true. Then write the number of the sentence(s) that best supports the answer.

   a. T F An electric current moves **a short distance through the circuit and then stops**. ____

   _____

   b. T F **An energy source, such as a battery**, can change electronic energy into light energy. ____

   _____

   c. T F **Closing a switch** on a circuit prevents the electric current from flowing. ____

   _____

   d. T F **A series circuit** is probably used to wire most schools. ____

   _____

2. In paragraph B, the word **components** most likely means:
   a. paths
   b. parts
   c. circuits
   d. electrons

3. A circuit containing four resistors all on the same path is:
   a. a simple circuit.
   b. a series circuit.
   c. a parallel circuit.
   d. all of the above

   Write the numbers of the two sentences that best support the answer. ____, ____

4. What type of circuit could have several paths?

   _____

   Write the number of the sentence that best supports the answer. ____

5. Complete the table below as you find the amount of current, resistance, or voltage for each circuit below.

Circuit	Volts	Ohms	Amps
A	64	8	
B	77		11
C		12	7
D	15		3
E		15	9
F	650	50	

6. Use the table from number five to complete the following questions.

   a. Which circuit has the most resistance?

   _____

   b. Which circuit has the most voltage?

   _____

   c. Which circuit has the least current?

   _____

   d. Which circuit has equal amounts of resistance and current?

   _____

Use the information from the lesson and the following symbols to complete the following circuit diagrams.

| Resistor | Battery |

7. Label the components on this simple circuit diagram in the box below:

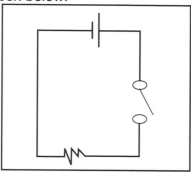

8. Draw a series circuit diagram with one battery and three resistors in the box below.

9. Draw a parallel circuit diagram with one battery, four resistors, and two switches in the box below.

Written Response Questions

For the following question, apply all of the information you have learned when answering.

10. Pretend that the parallel diagram that you drew in number nine is a diagram of a circuit in your bedroom at home. One of the resistors might be a radio in your room that transforms electric energy into sound energy. Tell what the other three resistors are symbols for and explain what type of energy they transform to.

_____

_____

_____

_____

_____

_____

_____

_____

_____

_____

14. Electromagnets

A [1]Recall for a moment where there are magnets in your home or school. [2]Most likely you are thinking of places with metal surfaces. [3]**Magnets** attract certain metals, such as nickel, iron, or cobalt. [4]A **permanent magnet** holds its magnetic properties over a long period of time. [5]All magnets have north-seeking and south-seeking poles. [6]When experimenting with two magnets, you have probably observed how the opposite poles attract each other and how like poles repel each other. [7]The area around a magnet that attracts or repels is known as the **magnetic field**. [8]Earth has a magnetic field around it due to what scientists believe are electric currents in the liquid metal layer around Earth's inner core. [9]You can observe this magnetic field using a compass, which will point to Earth's North Pole.

B [10]How are electricity and magnetism related? [11]In the year 1820, a Danish professor, Hans Christian Oersted, was demonstrating electric current in a wire to his class. [12]He happened to notice the needle in a nearby compass moved each time the electric current was turned on. [13]He had made the discovery that moving electric charges create a magnetic field, which became known as **electromagnetism**. [14]This discovery led to the creation of **electromagnets**, which are devices that become magnetic when an electric current flows through coiled wire in a circuit.

C [15]Examine the diagram below to see how easy it is to make an electromagnet. [16]Notice that a metal nail was placed inside the coiled wire, which makes the magnetism stronger.

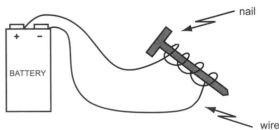

[17]How can the electromagnet be made even stronger? [18]Increasing the number of coils or increasing the current will strengthen the electromagnet.

D [19]Do you use electromagnets every day? [20]You probably do without even realizing it. [21]Televisions, music speakers, computers, hair dryers, doorbells, and more have electromagnets within their mechanisms. [22]Electromagnets are often more useful than common magnets. [23]One reason is that you can easily and quickly change the strength of the electromagnet. [24]In addition, the electromagnet can be turned on and off. [25]Strong electromagnets are often connected to cranes in junkyards to lift heavy scrap metal, such as junked cars. [26]Since an electromagnet can be turned on and off, the huge powerful one attached to the crane can easily lift and release a heavy car with just the flip of a switch.

E [27]Appliances, such as washers and dryers, have an electromagnet within their electric motors. [28]Electromagnets cause the spinning force in **electric motors**. [29]A small electric motor includes a permanent magnet around the electromagnet. [30]The electromagnet attracts and repels the surrounding magnet, causing the electromagnet to spin like a wheel. [31]Study the diagram below. [32]Notice in diagram (a) how the electromagnet is attracted to the permanent magnet and in (b) how it is repelled to continue the rotating motion, which keeps the current flowing in the electric motor.

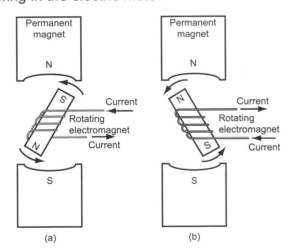

F [33]As you can see, electricity and magnetism are very closely related. [34]Scientists are continuously discovering new ways this relationship can advance electronic technology.

1. For each statement, circle T for true and F for false. If the statement is false, replace the **bold word(s)** to make the statement true. Then write the number of the sentence(s) that best supports the answer.

    a. T F   Electric motors function with **both permanent magnets and electromagnets**. ____

_____

    b. T F   Electromagnets are **very complicated devices** to make. ____

_____

    c. T F   An electromagnet is a **permanent magnet that creates electricity**. ____

_____

    d. T F   The south pole of a permanent magnet is **attracted to the north pole** of other permanent magnets. ____

_____

2. In paragraph D, the word **mechanisms** most likely means:
    a. large magnets
    b. outer casing of machines
    c. decorations on machines
    d. moving parts in machines

3. Electromagnets can be found:
    a. in computers.
    b. within electric motors.
    c. on cranes that lift heavy metal.
    d. all of the above

4. What are the two main benefits of using an electromagnet compared to a permanent magnet?

_____

_____

Write the numbers of the two sentences that best support the answer. ____, ____

5. Explain step-by-step how you could make an electromagnet.

_____

_____

_____

_____

Write the numbers of the two sentences that best support the answer. ____, ____

6. Show how magnets are attracted to each other by drawing a labeled diagram of two more permanent magnets attracted to the one below.

N	S

Write the numbers of the two sentences that best support the answer. ____, ____

Dawn conducted an experiment with an electromagnet that she made. Observe in the table below the changes she made to the electromagnet throughout the experiment.

How many paperclips can be lifted with an electromagnet?			
Number of coils wrapped around nail	3 volt battery	6 volt battery	12 volt battery
20	15	28	58
40	29	51	
80	57	99	

7. Dawn did not complete the last two data entries. After studying the results, estimate the amounts for the two parts left blank and complete the table with your estimated data.

8. What does this experiment prove about
   electromagnets made with different amounts
   of coils and different battery strength?

   _____   _____

   _____   _____

   _____   _____

   _____   _____

                                                 _____

Written Response Questions

For the following two questions, apply all of the information you have learned when answering.

9. Dennis made an electromagnet at home. He is able to pick up a small paperclip with his
   electromagnet.   However, when he tries to lift a large paperclip or napkin with his electromagnet,
   it doesn't seem to be working. What would you explain and recommend to Dennis to help him
   with this situation?

   _____

   _____

   _____

   _____

   _____

   _____

   _____

   _____

   _____

   _____

10. Explain two ways that electricity and magnetism are closely related.

   _____

   _____

   _____

   _____

   _____

   _____

   _____

   _____

   _____

   _____

   _____

15. Electric Energy

A [1]Many electronics use batteries to supply the power. [2]Batteries use **direct current** (**DC**) **electricity**. [3]Direct current is the continuous movement of electrons through a wire or other conducting material. [4]A chemical reaction in a battery causes the electrons to flow from the negative plate to the positive plate. [5]Scientifically, batteries are usually referred to as "cells." [6]A **wet cell** produces a current in a solution (liquid), and a **dry cell** produces a current with a moist paste. [7]A car battery is a good example of a wet cell: it contains a sulfuric acid solution. [8]Most of the batteries you use for electronic devices are carbon-zinc and alkaline dry cells.

B [9]The electricity that comes from the outlets in your home powers many electronics. [10]How does the electricity get to your home? [11]A **generator** changes mechanical energy into electrical energy. [12]A small generator is mainly composed of a coil of wire moving through a magnetic field, which generates electric current. [13]A **turbine**, which is a wheel connected to a long shaft that is attached to the coil, is used to turn the coil in some generators. [14]A source of energy, such as steam, is used to make the turbine move.

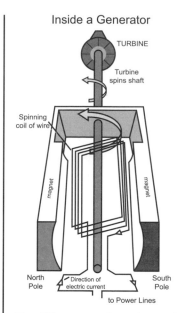

Inside a Generator

TURBINE

Turbine spins shaft

Spinning coil of wire

magnet

magnet

North Pole

Direction of electric current

South Pole

to Power Lines

C [15]Some generators use DC electricity, but most generators use **alternating current** (**AC**). [16]Alternating current reverses direction periodically. [17]The standard alternating current in the United States has a period of 1/60 seconds, meaning that the current completes 60 cycles each second.

D [18]A generator at an electric power plant supplies electrical power to an entire town using AC electricity. [19]A **transformer** is used to increase or decrease the voltage carried by the power lines. [20]High voltage lines will carry up to 10,000 volts (V). [21]For safety, a transformer will decrease the voltage to 1,200 V once those lines enter a residential area. [22]As the line reaches a home, a small transformer at the top of the last electric pole will decrease the voltage again to about 120 V.

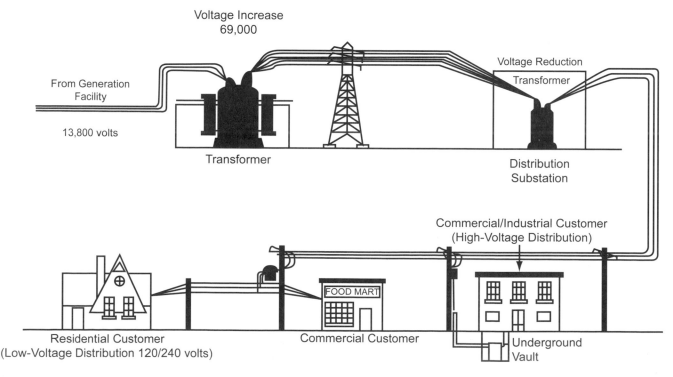

Voltage Increase
69,000

From Generation Facility

13,800 volts

Transformer

Voltage Reduction
Transformer

Distribution Substation

Commercial/Industrial Customer
(High-Voltage Distribution)

FOOD MART

Residential Customer
(Low-Voltage Distribution 120/240 volts)

Commercial Customer

Underground Vault

1. For each statement, circle T for true and F for false. If the statement is false, replace the **bold word(s)** to make the statement true. Then write the number of the sentence(s) that best supports the answer.

   a. T F   Wet cells and dry cells are **types of batteries**. _____

   _____

   b. T F   **All turbines** get energy from steam. _____

   _____

   c. T F   The batteries in radios and flashlights are most likely **dry cells**. _____

   _____

   d. T F   A transformer will **increase voltage** right before it enters your home. _____

   _____

2. In paragraph C, the word **periodically** means:
   a. recurring at equal intervals of time
   b. yearly
   c. monthly
   d. recurring at unequal intervals of time

3. In paragraph B, the word **generates** most likely means:
   a. electrifies
   b. eliminates
   c. alternates
   d. produces

4. Why is the electricity used in most generators called "alternating" current?

   _____

   _____

   _____

   Write the number of the sentence that best supports the answer. ____

5. Show your calculations for the following questions:

   a. How many cycles of standard alternating current does a generator complete in 10 seconds?

   _____

   _____

   b. How many cycles of standard alternating current does a generator complete in one minute?

   _____

   _____

   Write the number of the sentence that best supports the answer. ____

6. According to paragraph D, how much more electric power do high voltage power lines carry than residential power lines? (Show your calculations.)

   _____

   _____

Your home has an electric meter on it, which keeps track of how much electricity your family is using. The electricity is measured in kilowatt-hours. If you left a lamp on all day that has a 40-watt light bulb, it would use about one kilowatt-hour of electricity. Find out how much electricity your family is using in one day. First, write down the number on the electric meter. Then, 24 hours later, write down the number on the meter. Subtract the first number written from the second number written. This difference will show you the amount of electricity used in one day.

Carter's Home Electric Meter

732068	732174
Monday at noon	Tuesday at noon

7. What is the amount of electricity used by the Carter family in one day? (Show your calculation.)

_____

_____

_____

8. Give three examples of things you and your family could do to use less electricity.

_____

_____

_____

_____

Written Response Questions

For the following two questions, apply all of the information you have learned when answering.

9. Explain how a generator works. Begin with the turbine and then continue through the generator to the opposite end.

_____

_____

_____

_____

_____

_____

_____

_____

_____

_____

_____

10. Explain what a transformer does as electric current travels from high power lines to commercial power lines and then on to residential power lines.

_____

_____

_____

_____

_____

_____

_____

_____

_____

_____

_____

16. Energy Sources and Conversion

A [1]There are many different types of energy, such as energy from the sun, wind energy, light energy, sound energy, chemical energy, and many more. [2]Did you know that energy changes from one form to another through **energy conversion**? [3]For example, a flashlight converts the chemical energy in the battery to electric energy and then to light energy.

B [4]**Solar energy** is the first step in the sequence of many "energy chains." [5]Observe the flow chart below to see one example of how energy from the sun begins this sequence.

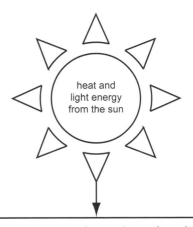

[6]The light energy transforms into chemical energy in plants to help them grow and produce food.

[7]People consume plants as food, which is converted into chemical energy in their bodies.

[8]The chemical energy in people's bodies can be converted to mechanical energy (muscle power).	[9]The chemical energy in people's bodies can be converted to heat energy (body temperature).

C [10]Even fuels that we burn for energy were derived from the sun's energy. [11]**Fossil fuels** such as coal, oil, and natural gas were formed from plant and animal remains that were buried under Earth's surface long ago. [12]The heat and pressure of Earth's crust converted these remains into fossil fuels. [13]Because it takes so long for fossil fuels to form, they are considered

nonrenewable resources. [14]This means we cannot get back these resources once they are used. [15]**Renewable resources** are energy sources that can be replenished in a short amount of time. [16]Hydropower (energy produced from flowing water), wind energy, solar energy, and biomass energy are all forms of renewable energy. [17]**Biomass energy** is formed using a method to convert plant and animal waste into fuels, such as ethyl alcohol and methane gas.

D [18]In addition to creating a method to produce fuels with biomass conversion, humans have also created devices to capture the energy from the sun and use it in beneficial ways. [19]Solar heat is probably the most commonly used type of convertible solar energy. [20]Many swimming pools are heated with solar panels that are usually attached to the roof of a building and angled toward the sun.

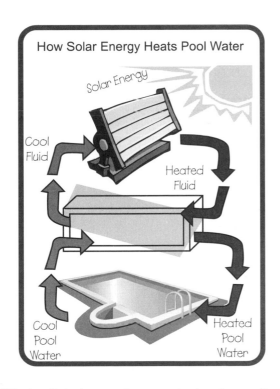

E [21]Scientists have also created **solar cells** that generate electricity from sunlight. [22]This electricity can be converted into energy to power vehicles, charge batteries, power motors, and to do much more.

F [23]As you can see, when energy is used, it is never lost completely; it only changes form.

1. For each statement, circle T for true and F for false. If the statement is false, replace the **bold word(s)** to make the statement true. Then write the number of the sentence(s) that best supports the answer.

   a. T F   Many things have been powered with **electricity using solar energy**. _____, _____

      _____

   b. T F   Energy can **only convert one time**. _____

      _____

   c. T F   Waste from cattle is used in **creating biomass energy**. _____

      _____

   d. T F   Energy is **gone after we use it**. _____

      _____

2. In paragraph C, the word **derived** most likely means:
   a. received from a source
   b. spread quickly
   c. taken apart.
   d. dissolved in water

3. In paragraph C, a synonym for the word **replenished** is:
   a. emptied
   b. used
   c. ruined
   d. refilled

4. How does food give you energy?

   _____

   _____

   _____

   _____

   Write the numbers of the sentences that best support the answer. _____, _____

5. Explain why this statement is **not** true: "It's okay to use a large amount of fossil fuels because they are found on Earth, so there's plenty to use."

   _____

   _____

   _____

   _____

   Write the numbers of the sentences that best support the answer. _____, _____

6. Referring to the solar heating diagram, explain the process of how solar panels heat pool water.

   _____

   _____

   _____

   _____

   _____

   _____
   | There is a type of flashlight that does not |
   | require batteries for energy. This flashlight |
   | has a crank handle instead. The crank |
   | flashlight creates electromagnetic energy. |
   | By rotating the crank for about one minute, |
   | the flashlight gives light energy for almost |
   | an hour. |
   _____

7. Why do you think the "crank flashlight" would be more beneficial compared to a battery-operated flashlight?

   _____

   _____

   _____

   _____

   _____

8. Fill in the flow chart below to show the type of energy that is converted when using the "crank flashlight."

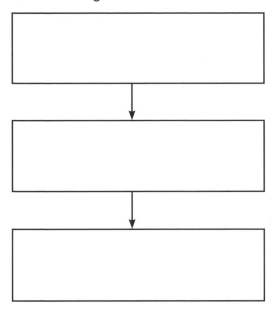

Written Response Questions

For the following two questions, apply all of the information you have learned when answering.

9. Invent a way to convert the energy from the sun into energy that would usually come from a different source. Explain this invention or draw a diagram.

_____

_____

_____

_____

_____

_____

_____

10. Explain how energy would be converted through an "energy chain" in order for you to have enough strength to move a heavy box.

_____

_____

_____

_____

_____

_____

_____

Unit II
LIFE SCIENCE

17. Cells

A [1]The **cell** is the basic unit of structure and function of all living things. [2]Cells work together to keep organisms alive. [3]Some organisms, such as bacteria, are only as big as a single cell. [4]Other organisms, animals, and humans are made up of many different kinds of cells. [5]Most cells, both plant and animal, range in size between 1 and 100 micrometers and are visible only with a microscope.

B [6]Robert Hooke, an English scientist, was the first to see actual cells. [7]In 1665, Hooke invented a microscope that helped him view and sketch the cells that made up a thinly sliced piece of cork. [8]The cork seemed to be made of little boxes, so he called them cells.

C [9]In 1673, another scientist, Anton van Leeuwenhoek, began studying single-celled living organisms. [10]Leeuwenhoek was the first to observe living single-celled bacteria and paramecia in great detail.

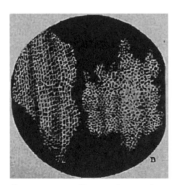

Cork cells as seen through a microscope.

D [11]By the 1800s, better microscopes were being made, and scientists were able to combine their studies of cells. [12]Their ideas were put together into a **theory**, which is an idea that is supported by data. [13]Two German scientists, Matthias Schleiden and Theodor Schwann, can be credited for The Cell Theory. [14]Together, they recognized and stated that all living things are made of cells.

E [15]About 15 years later, German scientist Rudolf Virchow concluded that cells didn't form on their own. [16]Scientists had thought that cells formed from air or nothing! [17]Virchow believed that cells divided from an existing cell to form new cells. [18]Discoveries and observations by many **histologists** (scientists who study cells) led to one of the major theories in science – **The Cell Theory**.

The Cell Theory states that:
- [19]All living things are made of one or more cells.
- [20]Cells are the basic units of living things.
- [21]All cells come from other cells.

F [22]All cells fall into one of two major classifications: prokaryotes and eukaryotes. [23]**Prokaryotes** were on Earth first and for billions of years were the only form of life. [24]They are single-celled organisms with no defined **nucleus** that can live on their own. [25]The nucleus is the largest, most visible part of a cell and is the control center of the cell's activities. [26]Bacteria and pond scum make up most of the prokaryotes classification.

G [27]**Eukaryotes** are more advanced than prokaryotes because each of their cells has a true nucleus inside a membrane. [28]In eukaryotic organisms, the nucleus is the largest, most visible part of the cell and is the control center of the cell's activities. [29]The **membrane** gives the cell its shape and helps control water and other substances that move in and out of the cell. [30]Eukaryotic organisms are usually multi-cellular organisms. [31]Plant and animal cells fall into this classification.

H [32]Although plant and animal cells are similar inside, there are major differences. [33]Plant cells can make their own food, but animal cells cannot. [34]Plants use a process called photosynthesis, which converts sunlight, water, and carbon dioxide into food energy (sugars and starches), oxygen, and water.

I [35]Another major difference is that while many animals have skeletal structures to provide support for their shape, plants rely only on cell walls for their form. [36]A cell wall is a nonliving, stiff outer covering that gives plant cells support and structure. [37]Without cell walls, flowers, plants, bushes, and trees would just flop over in a spongy mess!

1. For each statement, circle T for true and F for false. If the statement is false, replace the **bold word(s)** to make the statement true. Then write the number of the sentence(s) that best supports the answer.

   a. T   F   **Cells** are the basic unit of life.

   _____

   _____

   b. T   F   Anton van Leeuwenhoek was the first to observe **one-celled** living organisms. _____

   _____

   c. T   F   **Prokaryotes** are one-celled organisms with no defined nucleus. _____

   _____

   d. T   F   Plant cells have a stiff **cell wall** while animal cells do not. _____

   _____

2. What is the function of a cell's nucleus?
   a. converts sunlight, water, and carbon dioxide into food energy
   b. provides structure for the organism
   c. controls cell activity
   d. gives the cell its shape

   Write the number of the sentence that best supports the answer. _____

3. What is the most likely meaning of the word **defined** as it appears in paragraph F?
   a. explained
   b. specified
   c. exact meaning
   d. show the form or outline

4. According to the lesson, Robert Hooke invented a microscope to view cells. What other scientific information helped with developing The Cell Theory?

   _____

   _____

5. Refer to the lesson to explain the statement, "all cells are not created equal."

   _____

   _____

   _____

   _____

   _____

   Write the numbers of the three sentences that best support the answer.

   _____, _____, _____

6. Refer to paragraph E, which states The Cell Theory. Select one statement from The Cell Theory and explain it in your own words.

   _____

   _____

   _____

   _____

   _____

   In 1665, Robert Hooke observed cork cells through a microscope that he built. By 1838, Matthias Schleiden determined that every plant is made up of cells. In 1839, Theodor Schwann concluded that animals are also made up of cells. Since then, scientists have classified millions of plants and animals and, as different as they all are, every one of them is made of cells. Organisms that have many cells usually have many different kinds of cells within their structure. Each of these different cells has a different function.

7. Why do you think cells were not observed before the 1600s?

   _____

   _____

   _____

   _____

   _____

In the 1820s, Rene Dutrochet, a French biologist, studied plants and animals and determined that different parts of living organisms are made up of groups of cells. In many-celled organisms, these cells work in groups called tissues, which work together to perform the same function. Tissues that perform the same function are grouped together to form organs. Organs are then arranged into organ systems to perform certain functions.

8. Why are blood cells different from skin cells?

_____

_____

_____

_____

_____

Written Response Question

For the following two questions, apply all of the information you have learned when answering.

9.-10. Create a timeline of the discovery of cells. Label the dates. Include a brief description of the person and/or discovery.

_____

_____

_____

_____

_____

_____

_____

_____

_____

_____

_____

18. Cell Parts and Functions

A ¹What makes all plants and animals the same? ²They are made up of cells. ³Do you think they have the same kinds of cells? ⁴If you were to look at your cells and the cells of a plant, you would find that they have many characteristics in common.

Animal Cell

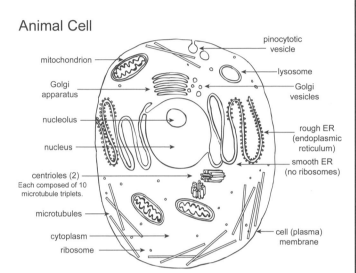

B ⁵All plant and animal cells have three main parts in common. ⁶Both have an outer covering, called a **cell membrane**, that gives the cell shape and helps control materials that move in and out of the cell. ⁷They also have a **nucleus**, which is the largest, most visible part of the cell. ⁸It is a round or egg-shaped structure found near the center of the cell and is usually darker in color than its surroundings. ⁹It contains DNA and controls all cell activities. ¹⁰All plant and animal cells also have **cytoplasm**, which is a gel-like substance inside the cell membrane that is primarily made up of water. ¹¹It also contains proteins, nutrients, and all of the other cell organelles.

C ¹²Animals and humans are made up of trillions of cells that are different sizes and shapes. ¹³Each of these cells contains a special nucleus membrane to protect the DNA and other advanced **organelles** (structures that perform specific tasks within the cell).

D ¹⁴All cells must perform certain functions in order to maintain life. ¹⁵Think of a cell operating like a factory. ¹⁶Every machine has to perform a specific job in order to make the factory run smoothly. ¹⁷Cells work the same way. ¹⁸Each part of the cell has a special job to make the cell work properly.

E ¹⁹The energy producers of the cells are the **mitochondria**. ²⁰They are rod-shaped structures that convert the chemical energy of food into a form that the cell can use.

Plant Cell

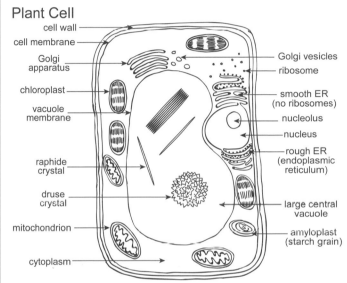

F ²¹The **vacuoles** are liquid-filled, sac-like storage spaces in cells. ²²They store food, water, and waste and help the cell digest food. ²³They also destroy viruses or bacteria that could damage the cell. ²⁴**Ribosomes** make protein for the cell under the direction of the nucleus. ²⁵Proteins are the building materials of the cell. ²⁶Ribosomes can be found along the edge of the cell's transportation system, which is called the **endoplasmic reticulum**. ²⁷**Lysosomes** contain powerful chemicals that break down harmful molecules and recycle worn-out cell parts.

G ²⁸Unlike animal cells, plant cells contain a nonliving structure called a cell wall and green, round shapes called chloroplasts. ²⁹The chloroplasts allow the plant to make its own food, primarily from sunlight.

1. For each statement, circle T for true and F for false. If the statement is false, replace the **bold word(s)** to make the statement true. Then write the number of the sentence(s) that best supports the answer.

   a. T F All plant and animal cells have a **nucleus**. _____

   _____

   b. T F **Organelles** are structures inside of animal cells that perform specific jobs inside the cell. _____

   _____

   c. T F **Animal** cells have a cell wall that helps support and protect the cell. _____

   _____

   d. T F **Chloroplasts** are organelles that make food for a plant. _____

   _____

2. What part of a cell controls the cell's activities?
   a. cell wall
   b. nucleus
   c. cellular membrane
   d. chloroplasts

   Write the number of the sentence that best supports the answer. _____

3. What is the basic unit of structure of all living things?
   a. a tissue
   b. an organ
   c. an organelle
   d. a cell

   Write the number of the sentence that best supports the answer. _____

4. Name the two structures found only in plant cells.

   _____

   _____

   _____

   Write the number of the sentence that best supports the answer. _____

5. Refer back to the lesson to explain the function of the nucleus in a cell.

   _____

   _____

   _____

   _____

   Write the number of the sentence that best supports the answer. _____

6. Apply what you read in paragraph B to explain the three main parts of plant and animal cells.

   _____

   _____

   _____

   _____

   Write the numbers of the sentences that best support the answer. _____, _____, _____

   Lysosomes, which are located in the cytoplasm of a cell, digest the food a cell takes in and get rid of the cell's wastes. Within the lysosome's spherical-shaped structure are chemicals that digest wastes and other cell parts that are no longer able to function. The membrane around each lysosome prevents the chemicals inside from breaking down the cell.

7. Explain the importance of the cell's membrane.

   _____

   _____

   _____

Living cells are made up of about 70 to 95 percent water. The diffusion of water in and out of a cell membrane is called osmosis. The water molecules will move from an area of greater concentration to an area of less concentration. When the concentrations are the same on each side of a cell membrane, a state of equilibrium, or balance, is reached. If there is more water leaving a cell than entering it, the cells will shrink and cause the plant to wilt.

8. What are some other examples of diffusion?

_____

_____

_____

_____

Written Response Questions

For the following two questions, apply all of the information you have learned when answering.

9. Use a Venn diagram to compare and contrast plant and animal cells.

Plant Cell   Animal Cell

10. Apply what you have read to explain how a cell works like a factory.

_____

_____

_____

_____

_____

_____

_____

_____

_____

_____

19. Reproduction and Growth of Cells

A [1]How do plants, animals, and you grow and develop? [2]In order for living organisms to grow, the number of their cells must increase through **reproduction**. [3]A cell reproduces by dividing into new cells. [4]Can you believe that you started out as a single cell?

B [5]How do plants and animals reproduce? [6]They can reproduce either **asexually**, where offspring come from a single parent, or **sexually**, where offspring are formed from the combination of sex cells from two parents.

C [7]**Asexual reproduction** is the simpler form of cell reproduction, since it requires only one parent. [8]One-celled organisms, such as bacteria, protozoa, and some plants, reproduce by simple cell division called **mitosis**. [9]The process of mitosis requires the cell to make a copy of its chromosomes, which are made up of DNA, so that the new cells will each have its own set of identical chromosomes. [10]Once there are two complete sets of chromosomes, the nucleus divides and then the entire cell divides. [11]In animals, the cell membrane pinches inward to create the two identical cells. [12]In plants, a new cell wall forms to divide one plant cell into two. [13]An organism that results from asexual reproduction is identical to its parent.

D [14]Cells from the top layer of your skin are constantly dying and being replaced with new skin cells. [15]In fact, the top layer of your skin will be replaced twice in one day! [16]All of your body cells replace themselves through the process of mitosis. [17]Whenever a cell divides, each new cell must receive an exact copy of the parent cell's chromosomes. [18]Having an identical set of chromosomes gives each new skin cell or body cell the same DNA code as its parent cell. [19]This makes sure that it will look and act like the older skin cells that it replaced.

E [20]Have you ever seen a mother dog and her puppy? [21]You may have noticed that the puppy didn't look exactly like its mother. [22]That is because dogs produce offspring by **sexual reproduction**, or reproduction by two parents. [23]The puppy inherits half of its DNA from one parent and half from the other. [24]Most organisms reproduce sexually.

F [25]Living things that reproduce sexually have special cells called sex cells. [26]The female parent has sex cells called **egg cells** and the male parent has sex cells called **sperm cells**. [27]These sex cells have only half as many chromosomes as the other cells in an organism's body. [28]A process called **meiosis** forms these sex cells. [29]In meiosis, one cell divides into four instead of two, so each new cell has half of the number of chromosomes as the original cell.

G [30]**Sexual reproduction** occurs when the male cell (the sperm cell) and the female cell (the egg cell) join together to form a new cell called a **zygote**. [31]This process is called **fertilization**. [32]The new zygote is the first cell of a new organism. [33]It has one complete set of chromosomes, half received from the male parent and half received from the female parent. [34]The zygote will continue to divide by mitosis to form the many cells that will make up the adult body of that organism.

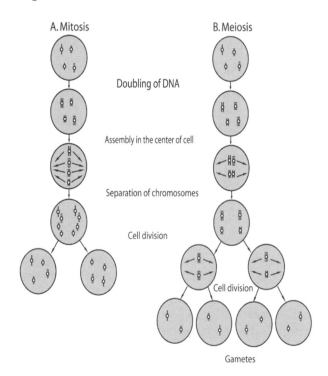

A. Mitosis

B. Meiosis

Doubling of DNA

Assembly in the center of cell

Separation of chromosomes

Cell division

Cell division

Gametes

1. For each statement, circle T for true and F for false. If the statement is false, replace the **bold word(s)** to make the statement true. Then write the number of the sentence(s) that best supports the answer.

   a. T   F   Humans start out as a **single** cell. _____

   _____

   b. T   F   The process of **mitosis** forms sex cells. _____

   _____

   c. T   F   Organisms that form as a result of **sexual** reproduction are identical to their parents. _____

   _____

   d. T   F   In **sexual reproduction**, the male cell and the female cell join together to form a new cell called a zygote. _____

   _____

2. Which word below could be used as a synonym for the word **results** in paragraph C?

   a. cause
   b. reply
   c. come from
   d. produce

   Write the number of the sentence that best supports the answer. _____

3. After meiosis, how does the number of chromosomes compare with the original number?

   a. remains the same
   b. half the number
   c. double the number
   d. triple the number

   Write the number of the sentence that best supports the answer. _____

4. Refer to the diagram of mitosis and meiosis. How do they differ?

   _____

   _____

   _____

   _____

5.-6. Create your own diagrams in order to demonstrate cell division in asexual reproduction and sexual reproduction.

Mutations are sudden changes that may occur in a gene or chromosome. These changes may affect the way traits are inherited. If a mutation occurs in a body cell, such as a bone cell, the mutation affects only the organism that has it. If the mutation occurs in a sex cell, then it can be passed on to an offspring. Some mutations are helpful and can be desirable in an offspring.

How do organisms grow? Food substances enter a cell through its membrane, and the cell uses this food to form new cell parts. When it reaches a certain size, it divides into two smaller cells. Many cells in your body are growing and dividing while some are dying. This is called the cell cycle. Cell division is a continuous cycle that every living organism is going through.

7. Imagine that you could create a useful mutation in a particular organism. What organism would you choose and why? How would that trait be useful?

_____

_____

_____

_____

_____

8. Compare the life cycles of a human and a cell.

Human	Cell

Written Response Questions

For the following two questions, apply all of the information you have learned when answering.

9. How did you grow from just one cell?

_____

_____

_____

_____

_____

_____

10. Apply what you have read to explain how mitosis can help to heal a wound.

_____

_____

_____

_____

_____

_____

20. Genetics

A [1]**Heredity** is the passing of traits from an organism to its offspring. [2]Traits that are passed on from parents to their offspring are called **inherited traits**. [3]The study of heredity is called **genetics**.

B [4]**Gregor Mendel**, the "father of genetics," began his experiments by growing different pea plants. [5]He observed that some pea plants were tall and some were short. [6]He also noticed that some produced green peas and others produced yellow peas. [7]In addition, the plants had either purple or white flowers.

C [8]His first experiment was to crossbreed two short-stemmed pea plants by pollination. [9]He discovered that when he planted the seeds from these plants, only short-stemmed plants grew.

D [10]Next, Mendel tried crossing two tall, or long-stemmed, pea plants. [11]He found that the tall pea plants did not always produce tall plants; the plants produced mostly tall and some short plants.

E [12]Mendel wondered what would happen if he took pollen from a pea plant that produced only tall plants and crossed it with a short-stemmed pea plant. [13]He discovered that all of the first generation plants were tall–there were no short plants at all!

F [14]Gregor Mendel's experiments led to basic principles of genetics, which state:
- [15]An organism receives two genes for each trait, one from each parent.
- [16]One of the genes may be stronger. [17]The trait of the stronger gene shows up and is called the **dominant gene**. [18]The trait of the weaker gene is "hidden," or does not show up, and is called the **recessive gene**.
- [19]An organism with genes that are alike for a particular trait is called a **purebred**.
- [20]An organism that has genes that are different for a trait is called a **hybrid**.

G [21]**Probability** can be used to predict genetic outcomes. [22]**Geneticists** (scientists who study genetics) use the laws of probability to predict the result of genetic crosses. [23]In addition to probability, a special chart called a Punnett Square is used to show the possible gene combinations in a cross between two organisms. [24]Reginald C. Punnett, an English geneticist, developed this chart.

H [25]A **Punnett Square** is a chart that shows all possible gene combinations in a cross of parents (see example below). [26]A capital, or uppercase, letter stands for the dominant gene (factor), and a lowercase letter stands for the recessive gene (factor). [27]The parents' genes are placed outside the square.

I [28]This Punnett Square predicts the traits of the offspring when a hybrid (Tt) tall plant is crossed with a purebred (tt) short plant. [29]According to the chart below, it is equally likely for the offspring plants to be hybrids (Tt) or purebreds (tt), since both appear the same number of times in the chart.

		Hybrid Tall Plant	
		T	t
Purebred **Short Plant**	t	Tt	tt
	t	Tt	tt

J [30]Some inherited traits do not follow Mendel's basic principles. [31]The two gene types for some traits are equally strong. [32]This pattern of inheritance is called **incomplete dominance**. [33]Incomplete dominance occurs when neither of the two forms of a trait completely masks the other. [34]In these traits, a blending of both traits shows up in the offspring.

K [35]For example, in some flowers, neither the red gene nor the white gene for flower color is dominant. [36]When these two genes are present in the same plant, a blending occurs. [37]What color do you think the offspring will be? [38]If you are thinking pink, then you are correct.

1. For each statement, circle T for true and F for false. If the statement is false, replace the **bold word(s)** to make the statement true. Then write the number of the sentence(s) that best supports the answer.

    a.   T   F   Heredity is the passing of traits from **parents** to offspring. ____

_____

    b.   T   F   An organism with two like genes for a trait is called **hybrid** for that trait. ____

_____

    c.   T   F Scientists who study heredity are called **plant breeders**. ____

_____

    d.   T   F A **hybrid** trait for tallness means you have one dominant trait for tallness and one recessive gene for shortness. ____

_____

2. What is the most likely meaning of the word **crossbreed** as it is used in paragraph C?
    a. plant
    b. reproduce a new plant by breeding two plants of different varieties or species
    c. make a duplicate plant
    d. reproduce a new plant by breeding two plants of the same variety or species

3. What is the most likely meaning of the word **masks** as it appears in paragraph J?
    a. a facial covering
    b. a mold of a person's face
    c. to cover or conceal
    d. to change appearance

4. Apply what you have learned about Punnett Squares in paragraphs H and I to predict the possible gene combinations of the offspring of a male and female guinea pig. The male guinea pig is a hybrid for the dominant gene of black fur (Bb). The female guinea pig is purebred for the recessive gene of brown fur (bb).

5. Using the Punnett Square in question 4:
    a. How many gene combinations are there? ____
    b. What color can the offspring be? Why?

_____

_____

_____

_____

    c. What is the probability that an offspring will be brown? ____
    d. What is the probability that an offspring will be black? ____

Every organism that reproduces sexually receives two genes for each trait. They receive one gene from each parent. That is why we usually look like our parents. The different forms a gene may have for a trait are called **alleles**. Most cells in our bodies have two alleles for every trait. If an organism has a pair of identical alleles for a trait, it is **homozygous** for that trait. If it has two different alleles for a trait, it is **heterozygous**.

6. For each genotype below, indicate whether it is heterozygous (He) or homozygous (Ho).

AA____   Bb____

Cc____   DD____

Ee____   ff____

The **genotype** is the genetic combination for a given trait, such as hair color. The genotype of each parent determines the hair color of the children. The **phenotype** is the actual physical trait an offspring has, such as hair color or eye color.

7. For each of the genotypes below, determine what phenotype would be possible. In the example, brown eyes (B) are dominant and blue eyes (b) are the recessive genes.

BB_____

Bb_____

bb_____

8. For each phenotype below, write the genotype. In this example, straight hair (S) is dominant over curly hair (s).

Straight_____ and _____

Curly_____

Written Response Questions

For the following two questions, apply all of the information you have learned when answering.

9. Explain what happened when Mendel crossed two tall pea plants. Write the letter of the paragraph that helped with this answer.

_____

_____

_____

_____

_____

_____

_____

_____

10. How is it possible for two parents, each with a dominant trait (E) for free earlobes, to have a child with the recessive trait (e) of attached earlobes? Draw a Punnett Square to help explain the answer.

_____

_____

_____

_____

_____

_____

_____

_____

21. DNA

A [1]Genes are made up of DNA (**Deoxyribonucleic Acid**), which contains the codes that tell each cell in the human body how to operate. [2]DNA is attached to the chromosomes.

B [3]A **chromosome** is a long strand in the nucleus, the control center for cells. [4]Chromosomes act like blueprints for transferring information to the next generation of cells. [5]This transfer takes place when the male cell joins with the female cell during reproduction. [6]When these cells join, they create a single cell that has two sets of chromosomes. [7]Humans have 2 complete sets of 23 chromosomes (2 X 23 = 46), one set from each parent.

C [8]How does DNA work? [9]If you picture DNA as a twisted ladder, it's easier to understand.

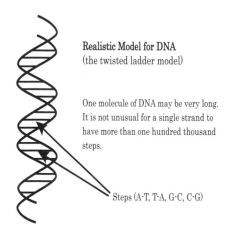

Realistic Model for DNA
(the twisted ladder model)

One molecule of DNA may be very long. It is not unusual for a single strand to have more than one hundred thousand steps.

Steps (A·T, T·A, G·C, C·G)

D [10]The steps of the ladder are made of chemical compounds called bases that fit together. [11]Geneticists created the 4-letter alphabet of DNA (A, T, C, G) from the first letter of each base compound. [12]Each step of the DNA staircase is made up of two base compounds: either A and T or G and C.

[13]For example, there might be an A – T, a G – C, a C – G, or a T – A. [14]This order can make many different combinations.

[15]The order in which the base compounds (letters) appear on the DNA "stairs" is the code that tells the cell how to function. [16]The letters (ATGCTCGAA…) create "words" (ATG CTC GAA…) which create "sentences" (<ATG CTC GAA TAA>…) that can be "read" on the genes.

E [17]If you know the base arrangement on one side, it is easy to reproduce the other side. [18]DNA duplicates itself by splitting down the middle to separate the bases. [19]Bases floating in the cell then pair with the appropriate separated bases to form two new DNA strands. [20]The two resulting DNA molecules are the same as the original one.

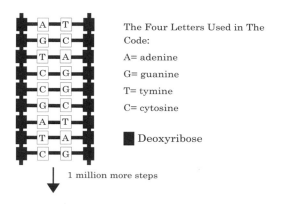

Simplified Model of DNA

The Four Letters Used in The Code:

A= adenine

G= guanine

T= tymine

C= cytosine

■ Deoxyribose

1 million more steps

F [21]The DNA in each cell of a particular organism is identical, but the DNA of every organism is different from that of every other organism. [22]The exception is **identical twins**, which are formed when one fertilized egg splits. [23]Identical twins are the only people (or animals) with identical DNA. [24]**Fraternal twins** do not have the same DNA because they are formed when two different eggs are fertilized.

[25]This means that if you think you are unique and nobody else has quite the same oddities, abilities, and problems … you are right!

1. For each statement, circle T for true and F for false. If the statement is false, replace the **bold word(s)** to make the statement true. Then write the number of the sentence(s) that best supports the answer.
    a. T F **DNA** contains the codes that tell each cell how to operate. ____

    _____

    b. T F **Genes** contain the DNA that tell each cell in the human body how to operate. ____

    _____

    c. T F Humans have one set of chromosomes from each of their parents, which gives them a total of **23** chromosomes. ____

    _____

    d. T F Identical twins are the only people (or animals) with **different** DNA. ____

    _____

2. What is the most likely meaning of the word **reproduce** as it is used in paragraph E?
    a. to recall or bring to mind again
    b. to make a copy
    c. to produce offspring
    d. to repeat after memorization

3. Which of the following is not part of the chemical compounds that make up DNA?
    a. A
    b. T
    c. G
    d. N

    Write the number of the sentence that best supports the answer. ____

4. Describe the structure of DNA.

    _____

    _____

    _____

    _____

Write the numbers of the sentences that best support the answer.

____, ____, ____

5. Refer to the diagrams and lesson to explain how DNA works.

    _____

    _____

    _____

    _____

6. Refer to paragraph B and explain the role of chromosomes in heredity.

    _____

    _____

    _____

    _____

Write the number of the sentence that best supports the answer. ____

Organisms with many cells are made up of body cells and sex cells. Skin cells, bone cells, tissues, and organs are composed of body cells. Roots and leaves of plants are also made of body cells. In fact, most of the cells in any organism are body cells. Adult organisms have sex organs, which produce sex cells.

7. What is the difference between body cells and sex cells?

    _____

    _____

    _____

    _____

8. After studying the lesson and diagrams, what do you suppose would happen if the base compounds on the DNA "staircase" did not copy the codes correctly? Explain your answer.

_____

_____

_____

_____

Written Response Questions

For the following two questions, apply all of the information you have learned when answering.

9. Apply what you have read to explain why identical twins have the same DNA.

_____

_____

_____

_____

_____

_____

_____

_____

_____

_____

10. Infer what you have read to support the idea that you are unique.

_____

_____

_____

_____

_____

_____

_____

_____

_____

_____

22. Uses of Genetics

A   [1]Have you ever seen a super mouse, a Frankenstein fish, or a square tomato? [2]Scientists have been using genetic engineering to improve medicine, plants, and animals for many years. [3]**Genetic engineering** is the process in which genes, or pieces of DNA, from one organism are transferred into another organism.

B   [4]Geneticists at the University of Pennsylvania were able to produce a super mouse by injecting it with a gene that has a protein called rat growth hormone. [5]The hormone causes the mouse to grow to twice its normal size—a super mouse!

C   [6]In 1985, scientists in China transferred a gene for human growth hormone into goldfish eggs. [7]Some of the goldfish grew two to four times their normal size. [8]In the United States, scientists transferred a growth gene from rainbow trout into another type of fish called carp. [9]These carp grew 20 to 40 percent larger than normal. [10]The offspring from these carp grew faster, too. [11]Scientists have been using genetic engineering to experiment with ways to make fish resistant to diseases and pollutants in the environment. [12]These experiments are beneficial for commercial fishermen and fish farming.

D   [13]How would you like a slice of a square tomato on your next sandwich? [14]These tomatoes have been created to have a square shape because they are easier to pick and package. [15]Many fruits and vegetables are more nutritious because genes that make the plant retain more vitamins and minerals have been spliced into the plant's genes. [16]**Gene splicing** is just what it sounds like: cutting the DNA of a gene from one organism and attaching it, or "splicing" it, to the genes of another organism. [17]You may be picturing sharp instruments and cutting, but this is not what happens. [18]Everything is done chemically.

E   [19]Scientists hope to find ways to cure diseases like cancer and diabetes through genetic engineering. [20]They are experimenting with ways to alter the genes that cause these diseases. [21]Vaccines have also been produced through genetic engineering. [22]When a vaccine is injected into a person's body, it reacts with the body to produce antibodies that protect a person from a certain disease.

F   [23]**Cloning** is another process using genetic engineering. [24]This process creates a genetically identical copy of an organism. [25]On February 22, 1997, people around the world were introduced to the first cloned lamb named Dolly. [26]Only one body cell from the parent was used to create Dolly's DNA.

G   [27]People have also been using **selective breeding** for centuries to produce better crops and healthier, hardier farm animals. [28]Selective breeding is the process of crossing plants or animals to produce offspring with specific desirable traits. [29]Farmers want plants that are more drought and insect resistant. [30]Many plants, such as corn and tomatoes, are bred for sweeter flavor and the ability to stay fresh longer.

H   [31]Selective breeding created most of the dog breeds we know today. [32]Many dog breeds, such as sheepdogs, were created to help round up livestock. [33]Some breeds, such as beagles, terriers, and other hunting dogs, were bred for their excellent sense of smell because it is helpful for tracking small game like rabbits and foxes. [34]Siberian huskies are useful for pulling sleds across the snow. [35]Their thick fur keeps them warm, and their strong, muscular build helps them to pull heavy loads.

1. For each statement, circle T for true and F for false. If the statement is false, replace the **bold word(s)** to make the statement true. Then write the number of the sentence(s) that best supports the answer.

   a. T   F Cutting the DNA of a gene from one organism and attaching it to the genes of another organism is known as **selective breeding**. _____

   _____

   b. T   F Selective breeding created most of the **dog breeds** we know today. _____

   _____

   c. T   F Many vaccines have been produced through **genetic engineering**. _____

   _____

   d. T   F The process of crossing plants or animals to produce offspring with certain traits is called **cross breeding**. _____

   _____

2. What is the meaning of the word **alter** as it is used in paragraph E?
   a. remove the ovaries
   b. insert words into text
   c. to change
   d. to cut out

3. Choose the best definition for the word **vaccine** as it is used in paragraph E.
   a. a substance prepared from dead or living bacteria or viruses that cause a disease that is injected into the body to prevent that particular disease
   b. a software program designed to detect and stop computer viruses
   c. inoculation
   d. prescription

4. Apply what you have learned from the lesson to explain how genetic engineering is useful.

   _____

   _____

_____

_____

Write the number of the sentence that best supports the answer. _____

5. Give two examples of the results of selective breeding.

   _____

   _____

   _____

   _____

6. What is gene splicing? How is it used?

   _____

   _____

   _____

   _____

   _____

Write the numbers of the sentences that best support the answer.

_____, _____, _____

People have been breeding plants and animals to produce certain traits for many years. This process is called **selective breeding**. Farmers have been selectively breeding chickens for many years. They will breed the hen that lays the most eggs. Many hens suffer from laying too many eggs. Their bones may become brittle because they use too much calcium to make all those eggs. This causes the hens to become weak and unable to access food. As a result they die at an early age. Our demand for cheap food has caused us to make our farm animals work harder. This is not always good for them.

Originally, dogs were used primarily for hunting, retrieving, or herding. The first step in selective breeding was to observe the dogs and select the ones that had the trait that was most desired. This trait may have been a keen sense of smell, great eyesight, or a thick coat. It also could have been a mixture of traits that made a dog attentive to sheep or cattle and/or a good guard dog. The second step would have been to breed that dog with another of the opposite sex that had the same desired trait. Most likely, the next generations would have the same desired traits.

7.-8. Use what you have read to decide whether or not you agree with selective breeding.

_____

_____

_____

_____

_____

_____

_____

Written Response Questions

For the following two questions, apply all of the information you have learned when answering.

9. Using information from the lesson, what do you think are the pros and cons of cloning animals?

_____

_____

_____

_____

_____

_____

_____

_____

_____

10. Does genetic engineering increase the nutritional value of foods? Explain.

_____

_____

_____

_____

_____

_____

_____

_____

23. Skeletal and Muscular Systems

A [1]The skeletal and muscular systems work together to give our bodies form, strength, and dexterity. [2]The skeletal system is made of living tissue, including blood vessels and nerve cells. [3]The skeletal system also provides support for our body, protects our internal organs, absorbs and stores important minerals for our bodies, and manufactures the red and white blood cells that are needed for our circulatory system.

B [4]The average adult skeleton is made up of 206 bones. [5]There are different types of bones, and each type has a purpose. [6]Long bones are light and strong and give our body the strength to support its own weight. [7]The bones of the arms and legs are long bones. [8]Short bones, such as those in the wrists and ankles, are small and allow the body to make flexible, defined movements and to maintain good balance. [9]Flat bones are made of two compact layers of bone that are separated by a spongy layer. [10]They are designed to protect the brain and the organs in the chest. [11]Many bones that make up the face, as well as the kneecaps and vertebrae, are irregular bones.

C [12]**Joints** are places where two bones meet. [13]Different kinds of joints allow our bodies to move in different ways. [14]**The ball-and-socket joints** let your limbs rotate, **pivot joints** allow for swiveling, and **hinge joints** permit a back-and-forth motion, like a hinge on a door. [15]**Fixed joints** connect bones together, like the bones in your face and skull. [16]They do not have any kind of motion.

D [17]Connective tissues hold everything together. [18]There are three types: ligaments, tendons, and cartilage. [19]**Ligaments** connect bone to bone, while **tendons** fasten muscle to bone. [20]The rubbery tissue called **cartilage** is used to bring bones together, to cushion bones, and to coat and protect the tips of bones at joints.

E [21]Working together, bones and muscles create movement. [22]There are three types of muscle fibers: **smooth** (involuntary), **cardiac**, and **striated** (voluntary). [23]All three are necessary in any activity, but striated muscles are the ones responsible for the movement of your arms and legs. [24]An electrical impulse sent from the brain stimulates the muscle, causing it to contract. [25]This shortens the muscle length, pulling the attached tendon, causing the bone to move. [26]You can see this action every time you flex your arm to show off your biceps. [27]Skeletal muscles, which move bones when we decide to move them, are **voluntary muscles**. [28]The cardiac muscle, which pumps the heart, and the smooth muscles in our blood vessels, stomach, and intestines are totally controlled by the nervous system and are **involuntary muscles**.

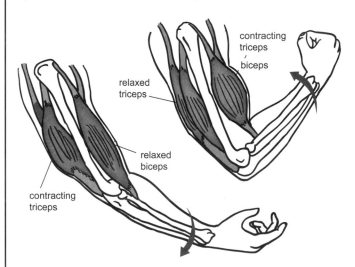

contracting triceps
biceps

relaxed triceps

relaxed biceps

contracting triceps

[29]The human body is so amazing and highly complex! [30]Together, the 206 bones and more than 600 muscles keep our fantastic "machine" in motion.

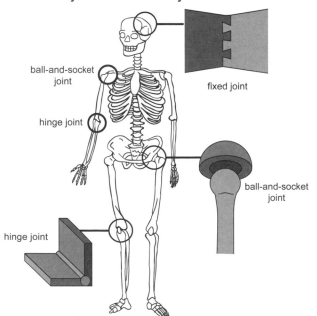

ball-and-socket joint

fixed joint

hinge joint

ball-and-socket joint

hinge joint

1. For each statement, circle T for true and F for false. If the statement is false, replace the **bold word(s)** to make the statement true. Then write the number of the sentence(s) that best supports the answer.

    a. T F Bones are attached to each other by **ligaments**. ____

    _____

    b. T F Bones meet at **joints**, where they are attached to each other and to muscles. ____

    _____

    c. T F **Involuntary muscles** move bones. ____

    _____

    d. T F The cardiac muscle, which pumps the heart, and the smooth muscles in our blood vessels, stomach, and intestines are controlled by the **voluntary muscles.** ____

    _____

2. Tendons are connective tissue that
    a. make blood cells.
    b. carry signals to the brain.
    c. connect one bone to another.
    d. connect a bone to a muscle.

    Write the number of the sentence that best supports the answer. ____

3. Choose the best definition of the word **compact** as it is used in paragraph B.
    a. having a short and solid stature
    b. closely and firmly packed together
    c. a small case containing a mirror and makeup
    d. loosely packed together

4. Apply information from the diagram and paragraph C to identify the different joints and distinguish how they function.

    _____

    _____

_____

_____

_____

5. Refer to the diagram of the arm muscles and paragraph E to describe the back-and-forth movement of your arm at your elbow.

    _____

    _____

    _____

    _____

    _____

6. Use the lesson and diagram to explain why voluntary muscles work in pairs.

    _____

    _____

    _____

    _____

    _____

There are two types of bone tissue: compact and spongy. **Compact bone** is made up of dense, circular layers of bone called **lamellae** and forms the outer layer of all bones. **Spongy bone** is made up of strong, light tissue, which is found in short, flat bones and in the ends of long bones. Every bone in your body is covered by **perisosteum,** which is a thin layer of tissue that contains cells for growth and repair. The bone itself is made up of blood vessels, nerves, and living bone cells called **osteocytes**, which are all located within a hard, non-living material containing calcium and phosphorus.

7. After reading the previous article and studying the diagram, compare the structures of compact and spongy bone tissue.

Compact	Spongy

Compact Bone & Spongy (Cancellous Bone)

Lacunae containing osteocytes
Lamellae
Canaliculi
Osteon
Periosteum
Osteon of compact bone
Trabeculae of spongy bone
Haversian canal
Volkmann's canal

Mammals have similar skeletal systems, but there are some differences due to their various adaptations. For example, some mammals have adaptations for flying.

8. Name two other mammals that have skeletal adaptations for survival.

_____

_____

Written Response Questions

For the following two questions, apply all of the information you have learned when answering.

9. Compare and contrast the different kinds of bones and their functions.

_____

_____

_____

_____

_____

_____

10. Describe the connective tissues of your skeleton.

_____

_____

_____

_____

_____

_____

24. Circulatory and Respiratory Systems

A ¹The circulatory and respiratory systems work together to deliver oxygen and other important nutrients to all of the cells in our bodies. ²The **circulatory system** is made up of blood, the heart, and blood vessels, such as arteries, veins, and capillaries. ³The **respiratory system** is responsible for bringing oxygen into the body from the air you breathe and then releasing carbon dioxide waste. ⁴It is made up of the lungs, nose, trachea, bronchial tubes, and alveoli.

B ⁵As air is inhaled through your nose and mouth, it travels down the **trachea,** or windpipe, and into two bronchial tubes. ⁶Each **bronchial tube** branches into one of our two lungs, where it divides into smaller and smaller branches, called **bronchioles**. ⁷At the end of the smallest tubes, the air reaches the millions of tiny balloon-like sacs, called **alveoli**. ⁸Each of the alveoli is surrounded by tiny blood vessels, called **capillaries**. ⁹This is where the oxygen-rich blood cells enter the body each time air is inhaled and where carbon dioxide is removed when air is exhaled.

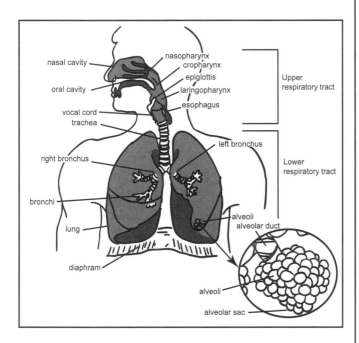

C ¹⁰The task of carrying the oxygen-rich blood to every cell in your body is assigned to the circulatory system. ¹¹Your heart pumps blood through your blood vessels to reach all parts of your body. ¹²The heart is a fist-sized muscle, which pumps an average of 70 times every minute. ¹³How many times would that be in one day? ¹⁴In one year? ¹⁵Your heart will beat about 3 billion times in your lifetime!

D ¹⁶The heart is divided into four **chambers**: the right atrium, the right ventricle, the left atrium, and the left ventricle. ¹⁷Very strong valves separate these chambers. ¹⁸The **right atrium** receives oxygen-poor blood from vessels called veins, and this blood is pumped into the **right ventricle**, which sends it to the lungs to pick up a fresh supply of oxygen. ¹⁹This oxygen-rich blood returns from the lungs to the **left atrium**, located at the top left side of the heart, and then it is pumped into the **left ventricle**. ²⁰From there it is pumped through vessels called arteries, which deliver oxygen and nutrients to all parts of the body. ²¹This pumping is the source of the heartbeat that can be heard and also felt when taking a pulse.

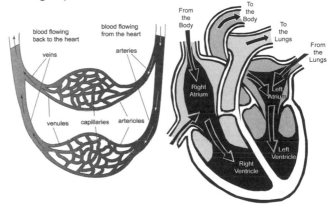

E ²²**Arteries** and **veins** branch out into smaller vessels called capillaries. ²³Capillary walls are so thin that oxygen, nutrients, and waste can pass right through them to enter and leave the cells in your body. ²⁴More than half of your blood is made of a yellowish fluid called **plasma**, which is 90% water and contains proteins, vitamins, and minerals. ²⁵The rest of the blood is made up of red blood cells, white blood cells, and platelets. ²⁶In a single drop of blood, there are about 5 million red cells, 8,000 white cells, and 250,000 platelets. ²⁷Red blood cells are made in the marrow of your bones and contain a protein called hemoglobin. ²⁸When oxygen is present in these cells, blood appears bright red. ²⁹White blood cells are very important disease-fighting forces that attack any intruders that invade the body. ³⁰Whenever our skin is cut or bruised, platelets create a scab with little protein threads called fibrin.

1. For each statement, circle T for true and F for false. If the statement is false, replace the **bold word(s)** to make the statement true. Then write the number of the sentence(s) that best supports the answer.

   a. T F Air that is inhaled through your nose and mouth travels down the **esophagus** and into the bronchial tubes. ____

   _____

   b. T F Blood cells are produced in the **heart**. ____

   _____

   c. T F The smallest blood vessels are the **capillaries**. ____

   _____

   d. T F **Alveoli** are tiny air sacs located at the ends of bronchi in the lungs. ____

   _____

2. What is the meaning of the word **chambers** as it is used in paragraph D?
   a. a room
   b. a compartment or enclosed space
   c. a hall for meetings
   d. a judicial or legislative body

3. What is the meaning of the word **intruder** as it is used in paragraph E?
   a. forceful people
   b. interfering signals
   c. unwanted cells
   d. improperly made cells

4. Apply what you have read from the lesson to compare the function of red and white blood cells.

Red cells	White cells

Write the numbers of the sentences that best support the answer. ____ , ____

5. Study the lesson to describe the path your blood travels around your body.

   _____

   _____

   _____

   _____

   _____

   _____

6. Refer to the diagram and lesson to describe what happens in the alveoli.

   _____

   _____

   _____

   _____

   _____

   _____

Write the numbers of the sentences that best support the answer.

____, ____, ____

Everyone's blood appears to be the same, but when it's examined under a microscope, differences are clear. Blood is divided into four main groups which are labeled A, B, O, and AB. In a blood transfusion, the type of blood you are given depends on the blood group to which you belong. A person with type A blood can donate blood to a person with type A or type AB. A person with type AB blood can donate blood to a person with type AB only. A person with type O blood can donate to anyone. Do you know your blood type?

7. Suppose a person required a blood transfusion. Why do you think it's important to receive the correct blood type?

_____

_____

_____

_____

8. There is a flap of skin called the epiglottis that is located between the trachea and the esophagus.

   What do you think is the purpose of the epiglottis?

_____

_____

_____

_____

_____

Written Response Questions

For the following two questions, apply all of the information you have learned when answering.

9. What is the relationship between the respiratory and circulatory system?

_____

_____

_____

_____

_____

_____

_____

_____

_____

10. Platelets in the blood cause clotting. Why is this important?

_____

_____

_____

_____

_____

_____

_____

_____

25. Nervous System

A [1]The central nervous system and the peripheral nervous system are the two major divisions of the nervous system. [2]The **central nervous system** consists of the brain and the spinal cord. [3]The brain controls body functions by sending and receiving messages through the spinal cord. [4]The **peripheral nervous system** consists of the sensory organs and body nerves. [5]**Nerves** are bundles of nerve cells, or neurons. [6]A **neuron** is a cell that can send signals to and receive signals from other neurons.

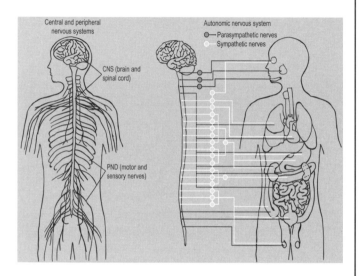

B [7]The **brain** is the most complex organ in the body and is the body's control center. [8]It sends messages to and receives them from all parts of the body. [9]Different areas of the brain control different body functions. [10]Near the back of the skull is the **cerebellum**, which controls the body's movements, balance, and posture. [11]Deep inside the brain is the **thalamus**, which is the destination for incoming messages from the rest of the body. [12]It sends out feelings of pain, touch, and temperature to other parts of the brain.

C [13]Around the thalamus is the **hypothalamus**, which controls involuntary body operations, such as heartbeat and blood circulation. [14]The pituitary gland is attached to the hypothalamus. [15]It controls most of the hormones in the body.

D [16]The **cerebral cortex** covers the central parts of the brain and is made up of two cerebral hemispheres. [17]The nerve centers that control thought and voluntary action are located in these hemispheres. [18]Nerve fibers from the two cerebral hemispheres cross one another in a part of the brain called the medulla before they move down the spinal cord. [19]Each hemisphere usually controls functions in the opposite side of the body. [20]For example, a region in the left hemisphere controls movement of the right arm.

E [21]Once messages leave the central nervous system, they are carried by the peripheral nervous system. [22]The peripheral system includes the **cranial nerves** (nerves that branch from the brain) and the **spinal nerves** (nerves that branch from the spinal cord). [23]These nerves send sensory messages from receptor cells in the body to the central nervous system. [24]**Receptor cells** are nerve cells that identify conditions in the body's environment. [25]For example, receptors in the ears detect sound waves, while receptors in the skin detect heat, cold, and feelings from touch.

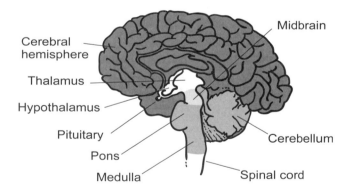

F [26]The **autonomic nervous system** is also part of the peripheral nervous system. [27]It controls muscle actions that are automatic responses to situations. [28]These are called **reflexes**. [29]Reflexes protect the body from things that can harm it. [30]For example, if you put your hand on a hot stove, a reflex causes you to quickly remove your hand. [31]A message of pain is sent to the spinal cord that relays it to a nerve traveling to the brain. [32]The nerve from the spinal cord quickly sends a message back to the muscle in your hand to remove it from the stove. [33]The reflex action of the muscles to avoid the source of pain happens even before the signal reaches the brain, meaning you react to pain before you even feel it.

1. For each statement, circle T for true and F for false. If the statement is false, replace the **bold word(s)** to make the statement true. Then write the number of the sentence(s) that best supports the answer.

    a. T F The **heart** is the most complex organ in the body. _____

    _____

    b. T F The **peripheral nervous system** consists of the sensory organs and body nerves. _____

    _____

    c. T F The **pituitary gland** is attached to the hypothalamus and controls most of the hormones in the body. ___, ___

    _____

    d. T F The brain controls body functions by sending and receiving messages through the **back bone**. _____

    _____

2. Which of the following is **not** part of the nervous system?
    a. autonomic nervous system
    b. peripheral nervous system
    c. central nervous system
    d. they all belong to the nervous system

    Write the numbers of the sentences that best support the answer.

    _____, _____, _____

3. The brain can do which of the following?
    a. receive information
    b. cause movement
    c. think and learn
    d. all of the above

    Write the numbers of the sentences that best support the answer.

    _____, _____, _____

4. What are nerves?

    _____

    _____

    _____

    _____

Write the numbers of the sentences that best support the answer. _____, _____

5. Do parts of your brain perform specialized functions? If so, give at least two examples.

    _____

    _____

    _____

    _____

6. Refer to the lesson to explain the relationship between the central nervous system and the other systems of your body.

    _____

    _____

    _____

    _____

    _____

Messages travel along neurons in the form of electrical signals called nerve impulses. When an impulse reaches the gap, or **synapse**, between one neuron and the next, a chemical is released and helps carry the signal to the next neuron.

7. Refer to the diagram and text to explain, in your own words, how a neuron transmits signals.

    _____

    _____

    _____

    _____

    _____

Have you ever wondered why it hurts when you hit your "funny" bone? Your funny bone is actually located at a place where a nerve crosses over the surface of the humerus bone, which is your elbow.

8. Now explain what happens to let you know that your elbow hurts.

_____

_____

_____

_____

Written Response Questions

For the following two questions, apply all of the information you have learned when answering.

9. Apply what you have read to trace the path that nerves use to pass along messages to the brain.

_____

_____

_____

_____

_____

_____

_____

_____

10. Why are your brain and central nervous system important in your everyday life?

_____

_____

_____

_____

_____

_____

_____

_____

26. Digestive System

A [1]Think for a moment about a favorite food you might have for dinner. [2]Before you take that first bite, your digestive system begins its work. [3]Glands in your mouth produce **saliva** when you start thinking about the food you're about to eat. [4]Saliva moistens the food and breaks it down to make it soft and easy to swallow.

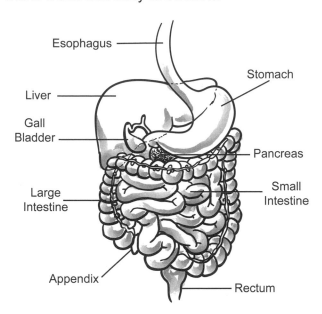

Esophagus

Liver

Gall
Bladder

Large
Intestine

Appendix

Stomach

Pancreas

Small
Intestine

Rectum

B [5]When you swallow, the food passes through the **esophagus**, which is a tube that is approximately 10 inches long. [6]There the walls of the esophagus contract slowly to squeeze the food down into the **stomach**. [7]This process only takes only about 2 or 3 seconds.

C [8]Your stomach is a large, sack-like organ that produces gastric juices, which are made of acid and other chemicals that help to break down the food into a liquid mixture called chyme. [9]The gastric juices include hydrochloric acid, which also helps kill bacteria that might be in the food you ate. [10]After several hours in the stomach, the liquid food slowly moves into the **small intestine**.

D [11]Your small intestine has three sections: the duodenum, the jejunum, and the ileum. [12]The first part of the small intestine is the **duodenum**. [13]It receives the partially digested food from the stomach and begins the absorption of nutrients for your body. [14]This is where digestive juices from the liver and pancreas help break down the fats, protein, and starch in the food before it passes to the jejunum. [15]The **jejunum** is the coiled middle section of the small intestine. [16]The third and final section of the small intestine is the **ileum**. [17]An adult's small intestine would be about 22 feet in length if it was stretched end to end.

E [18]The inner wall of the small intestine is covered with millions of microscopic, finger-like projections called **villi**. [19]The **villi** are small projections that stick out of the walls of the small intestine to absorb nutrients into the blood. [20]The nutrient-rich blood is then carried to your liver for more processing before it is carried around your body. [21]Your food may be in your small intestine for about four hours before the indigestible food continues into the large intestine.

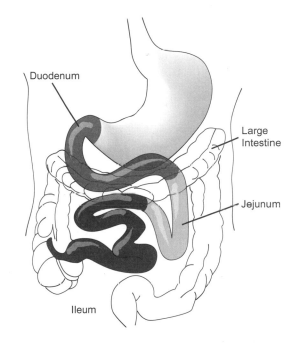

Duodenum

Large
Intestine

Jejunum

Ileum

F [22]Your large intestine is about 3 or 4 inches around and would measure about 5 feet long if you spread it out. [23]Water and any food that cannot be digested move into the first part of the large intestine, called the **colon**. [24]There, any remaining water and some minerals are absorbed into your bloodstream. [25]After most of the nutrients are removed from the food mixture, there is waste left over that your body can't use. [26]This somewhat solid waste matter, called feces, then passes into the second part of the large intestine, called the **rectum**, where it remains until you are ready to go to the bathroom. [27]Next time you have that dinner you were thinking about, you'll know where it goes!

1. For each statement, circle T for true and F for false. If the statement is false, replace the **bold word(s)** to make the statement true. Then write the number of the sentence(s) that best supports the answer.

   a. T F Chemicals in the stomach help break down food into a liquid called **hydrochloric acid**. _____

   _____

   b. T F The **stomach** helps break down fats, protein, and starch in the food. _____

   _____

   c. T F An adult's **large intestine** could be about 22 feet in length if it was stretched out. _____

   _____

   d. T F **Villi** are small projections in the small intestine that absorb nutrients into the blood. _____

   _____

2. What is the most likely meaning of the word **absorption** as it appears in paragraph D?
   a. a state of mental concentration
   b. uptake of substances by a tissue
   c. preoccupation
   d. the removal of energy or particles from a beam

3. Which word would be a <u>synonym</u> for the word **projections** as used in paragraph E?
   a. protrusions
   b. projects
   c. overhangs
   d. predictions

4. Label the main organs of the digestive system.

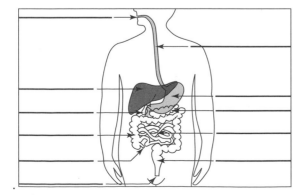

5. Why is digestion important?

   _____

   _____

   _____

   _____

6. Explain the function of the stomach.

   _____

   _____

   _____

   _____

   Write the numbers of the sentences that best support the answer.

   _____, _____, _____

   The digestive system also works with other systems in the body such as the circulatory system, which helps distribute the nutrients to the body through blood cells. The endocrine system helps control the speed of digestion, while the excretory system filters wastes from the bloodstream and collects them in urine.

7. In your opinion, which organ plays the most important role for the digestion of food? Explain.

   _____

   _____

   _____

   _____

   _____

The digestive system has its own way of controlling the digestive process. The major hormones that control the functions of the digestive system are produced by the stomach and small intestine. These hormones are released into the blood of the digestive tract and travel through the arteries. Then they return to the digestive system where they cause the digestive juices to flow, which helps the digestive organs do their jobs. These hormones work with the brain to regulate the intake of food to provide energy.

8. What information would you use to support the idea that it's important to control the digestive process?

_____

_____

_____

_____

_____

_____

Written Response Questions

For the following two questions, apply all of the information you have learned when answering.

9. Imagine that you just took a bite of an apple. Use the answers from question 4 and the lesson to explain the digestion of a bite of apple and what happens in each organ.

_____

_____

_____

_____

_____

_____

_____

_____

10. What information would you use about digestion to make future decisions about your food choices?

_____

_____

_____

_____

_____

_____

_____

27. Reproductive System

A [1]The process that a living organism uses to produce more of its own kind is called **reproduction**. [2]Humans may live long and healthy lives without reproducing offspring, but if our species is to continue, some people must reproduce.

B [3]The human **reproductive system** is made up of the parts of the body that are involved in creating new life. [4]It has four functions:
1. to produce egg and sperm cells.
2. to move and support these cells.
3. to nourish the developing offspring.
4. to produce hormones.

C [5]In many animals, the male's body makes male sex cells, or **sperm**, and a female's body produces **ova,** or **egg cells**. [6]In some animals, such as reptiles and mammals, **sexual reproduction** occurs when a sperm cell meets with an ovum in the female's body to form a new cell in a process called **internal fertilization**. [7]The main purpose of **fertilization** is to join the sperm and egg cell to create offspring.

D [8]In many animals, such as amphibians and fish, fertilization happens outside of the body. [9]The female will lay her eggs, and then the male will later spray his sperm over the eggs to fertilize them. [10]This is called **external fertilization**.

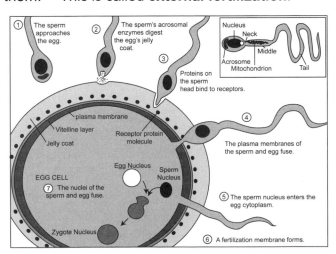

E [11]The new cell that is formed in reproduction is called a fertilized egg, or **zygote**, and it is the first cell of a new offspring. [12]It continues to divide by mitosis. [13]The zygote develops and grows into a new animal or human.

F [14]Animals and plants all have different numbers of chromosomes. [15]Humans have 46 chromosomes in each of their body cells. [16]A human sperm cell and ovum have 23 chromosomes each. [17]When they join, they become one cell with 46 chromosomes; fertilization makes sure that each cell of the new offspring has the same number of chromosomes as in each cell of the parents. [18]This cell will divide many times through **mitosis** to form an individual.

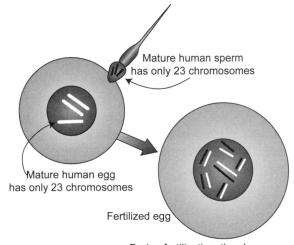

Mature human sperm has only 23 chromosomes

Mature human egg has only 23 chromosomes

Fertilized egg

During fertilization, the chromosomes from the sperm and egg unite to give the fertilized egg (also called a zygote) a total of 46 chromosomes.

G [19]As the cell divides, the new cells grow into different types of cells, such as bone cells, blood cells, and skin cells. [20]Cells of the same type join together to form **tissues**. [21]Different tissues form **organs**, and organs group together to form **systems**.

H [22]Sex cells are formed differently than body cells. [23]Sex cells are formed in a process called **meiosis**, where the nucleus of a sex cell divides twice, making four new cells that each have half the number of original chromosomes. [24]Meiosis is very important because it makes sexual reproduction possible.

I [25]From the time we are teenagers through mid-life or longer, we are capable of sexually reproducing. [26]The human female needs a male to fertilize her egg, even though she is the one who carries the baby through pregnancy and childbirth.

1. For each statement, circle T for true and F for false. If the statement is false, replace the **bold word(s)** to make the statement true. Then write the number of the sentence(s) that best supports the answer.

   a. T F **External fertilization** occurs outside of an animal's body. _____

   _____

   b. T F A human sperm cell and ovum have **23** chromosomes each. _____

   _____

   c. T F The new cell that is formed in reproduction is called a fertilized **gene**. _____

   _____

   d. T F Sex cells form through a process called **meiosis**. _____

   _____

2. Which one is **not** a function of the human reproductive system?
   a. to produce sperm and egg cells
   b. to nourish the developing offspring
   c. to produce hormones
   d. None of the above–they are all a function of the reproductive system.

   Write the number of the sentence that best supports the answer. _____

3. Which word below would be a <u>synonym</u> for **develops** as used in paragraph E?
   a. intensifies
   b. expands
   c. progresses
   d. acquires

4. Apply what you have learned from the graphics and lesson to compare the difference between meiosis and mitosis. Use a compare and contrast chart.

mitosis	meiosis

5. Refer to the lesson to explain reproduction and its importance.

   _____

   _____

   _____

   _____

   _____

   Write the number of the sentence that best support the answer. _____

6. Explain how fish use external fertilization.

   _____

   _____

   _____

   Write the number of the sentence that best supports the answer. _____

   > Life expectancy is the average time an individual organism might live according to the conditions of its environment. These conditions are determined by the availability of food, water, and shelter. The life span of an organism is the average length of time an organism can live under the best conditions. This means it always has a continued supply of food, water, and good shelter.

7. Why do you think life expectancy depends on where you live?

   _____

   _____

   _____

   _____

Plants go through the life cycle just as animals and cells do. A tree is made of millions of cells that use the cell cycle to grow and replace worn out or dead cells. It uses the reproductive cycle to make more trees. Animals go through the life cycle, too, whether they are single-celled organisms or people. They are born, grow, sometimes reproduce, and then die.

8. How would you compare the cell cycle, the reproductive cycle, and the life cycle?

_____

_____

_____

_____

_____

Written Response Questions

For the following two questions, apply all of the information you have learned when answering.

9. Humans have 46 chromosomes in each of their body cells. Is this statement always true, sometimes true, or never true? Explain.

_____

_____

_____

_____

_____

_____

_____

_____

10. What is the importance of meiosis?

_____

_____

_____

_____

_____

_____

_____

_____

_____

28. Classification of Organisms

A [1]All living things were first classified into one of only two groups: the plant group or the animal group. [2]Then, with the invention of the microscope in the 17th century, scientists were able to observe organisms much more closely. [3]This resulted in many new discoveries about organisms, necessitating the addition of four classifications to the two original ones. [4]These are now known as the six kingdoms; **archaebacteria**, **eubacteria**, **protists**, **fungi**, **plants**, and **animals**. [5]Members of each kingdom can be further separated into smaller groups using their characteristics.

B [6]The **animal kingdom** is divided into very specific categories. [7]This hierarchy is most specific at the bottom with **species**, which are able to interbreed and produce fertile offspring. [8]The tiers then become broader with **genus**, **family**, **order**, **class**, **phylum**, and **kingdom**.

C [9]To understand the animal kingdom better, let's see how the grizzly bear is classified. [10]To be very specific, the grizzly bear, scientifically known as Horribilis, is a sub-species of the brown bear species, scientifically known as Ursus Arctos. [11]This species includes other brown bears, such as the Kodiak bear and the Mexican brown bear. [12]The genus Ursus includes all brown bears, black bears, the polar bear, and more. [13]The bear family, scientifically known as Ursidae, is even broader and includes the panda bear. [14]All of these animals in the Uridea family share common characteristics, such as a large body, stocky legs, a long snout, shaggy hair, non-retractable claws, and a short tail. [15]The Carnivora order comes next and includes all carnivorous (meat–eating) mammals. [16]The mammalia class of animals are all vertebrates, are warm-blooded, have hair or fur, and the females have mammary (milk-producing) glands. [17]The Chordata phylum is a very extensive group that includes all vertebrates and even some invertebrates. [18]Finally, there is the animal kingdom, which includes all animals and even insects from the arthropoda phylum and sponges from the Porifera phylum.

D [19]Like the members of the animal kingdom, the organisms in the plant kingdom are multicellular. [20]However, they differ from one another because plants make their own food,

whereas animals obtain their food by ingesting other living things, including plants. [21]All plants can be divided into two groups: vascular and nonvascular. [22]The **vascular** plants circulate food and water through the plant, which can cause these plants to grow quite large. [23]The **nonvascular** plants are not able to grow very large because they do not have the special tube-like tissues for circulation. [24]Instead, the non-vascular plants pass these materials slowly from one cell to the next. [25]Study the diagram below to see how plants are classified into even more specific groups.

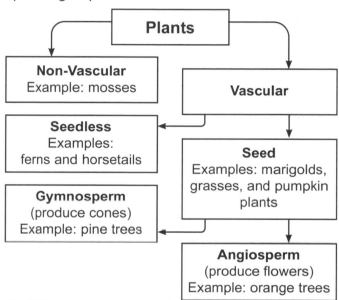

E [26]The fungi kingdom is a group of organisms that grow in dark, moist areas and look similar to plants. [27]To get energy, fungi take in nutrients from other organisms. [28]Mold that grows on a piece of fruit is one example of fungi. [29]Other common fungi are yeast and mushrooms.

F [30]The protists kingdom is made of organisms that cannot be classified into any other kingdom. [31]The plant-like protists, algae, make their own food. [32]The animal-like protists, protozoa, take in food from their surroundings.

G [33]All bacteria are **microbes**, meaning they can only be seen with a microscope. [34]Bacteria are divided into two kingdoms. [35]The archaebacteria are considered "ancient bacteria" because they have been able to survive through extreme hot and cold conditions. [36]Eubacteria are the more common bacteria found almost everywhere, including in soil and people.

1. For each statement, circle T for true and F for false. If the statement is false, replace the **bold word(s)** to make the statement true. Then write the number of the sentence(s) that best supports the answer.

   a. T F Two animals able to reproduce together are in the same **species**.
   ____

   _____

   b. T F All bears are in the same **genus** and share common characteristics. ____, ____

   _____

   c. T F Vascular plants grow to **the same size as** nonvascular plants. ____, ____

   _____

   d. T F Archaebacteria and eubacteria are **microscopic**. ____

   _____

2. What part of an animal's body is comparable to the vascular plant's tube-like tissues?
   a. hair
   b. skin
   c. bones
   d. veins

3. In paragraph B, the word **tiers** most likely means:
   a. series of rows placed one above the other
   b. broken pieces
   c. sad emotions
   d. wide circular items

4. Why do fungi grow on other organisms?
   a. to kill it
   b. to get energy
   c. to stay warm
   d. for protection

   Write the number of the sentence that best supports the answer. ____

5. Complete the chart below to give examples of these four kingdoms.

Kingdoms			
Animals	**Plants**	**Fungi**	**Protists**
ducks	oak trees	yeast	
spiders	tomato plant		

6. Some bacteria can make us sick, yet other bacteria can keep us healthy. No matter how well we wash our hands, we always have some bacteria left on our hands. Which kingdom does this type of bacteria probably belong to?

   _____

   Write the number of the sentence that best supports the answer. ____

7. Which class of animals are humans a part of?

   _____

   List a few characteristics to support the answer:

   _____

8. Fish make up the largest class of vertebrate.

   List a few characteristics that all species of fish have in common.

   _____

   _____

   _____

   _____

9. Demonstrate your understanding of how the grizzly bear is classified on this hierarchy chart. Fill in the blank with the name of each classification. Then, along with the grizzly bear, add as many other examples as possible for each tier.

Kingdom: _____
Examples:

Phylum: _____
Examples:

Class: _____
Examples:

Order: _____
Examples:

Family: _____
Examples:

Genus: _____
Examples:

Species: _____
Examples:

Sub-Species

_____

Written Response Question

For the following question, apply all of the information you have learned when answering.

10. Explain how plants are classified into specific groups.

_____

_____

_____

_____

_____

_____

_____

_____

_____

_____

_____

29. Function of Plant Parts

A [1]Think about all the plants you see daily. [2]The majority of these plants are **vascular**, which means they are able to circulate water and nutrients throughout their parts. [3]The vessels, or tubes, used for circulation run through the roots, stems, and leaves of the plant.

B [4]The **roots** usually grow below the ground to hold the plant in place and to absorb water and minerals from the soil. [5]These substances enter the root through a thin layer of cells called the **epidermis**. [6]Next they travel to the **xylem**, which is a strong vessel that transports the water and minerals from the roots to other parts of the plant. [7]The **phloem** is another vessel that is thinner and carries **glucose**, which is the sugary food made in the leaves, to other parts of the plant. [8]Some plants, like the potato plant, store a large amount of food in their roots.

C [9]A thin, delicate flower stem and a wide, hard tree trunk are both considered **stems**, which have one main job: to support the plant. [10]The xylem and the phloem move nutrients through the stem to the leaves. [11]Study the diagram below. [12]It shows what you might see if you looked at a cut section of a leaf under a microscope.

D [13]You have probably seen **leaves** in a variety of shapes and sizes. [14]All leaves have the very important job of performing **photosynthesis**, which is the process of converting water, sunlight, and carbon dioxide into food for the plant in the form of glucose (sugar) and starch. [15]The water and gases flow into the leaf's epidermis through small holes, known as **stomata**. [16]A pair of **guard cells** surrounds each stoma. [17]These cells open and close the stoma. [18]Sunlight causes the guard cells to open, so they are usually open during the day and closed at night. [19]**Chlorophyll**, which is a green pigment within the plant cells, absorbs the light energy that reaches the leaf, enabling the plant to make glucose. [20]Find the **mesophyll** in the diagram below. [21]The majority of the chlorophyll is in the mesophyll. [22]Oxygen, which all living organisms rely on, is a byproduct produced during photosynthesis.

E [23]**Transpiration** occurs during photosynthesis, causing the leaf to lose water when the stoma is opened. [24]As long as the xylem has enough water, it will transport more water up to the leaf. [25]However, when the xylem is not filled with water due to the ground soil being too dry, the leaves will wilt.

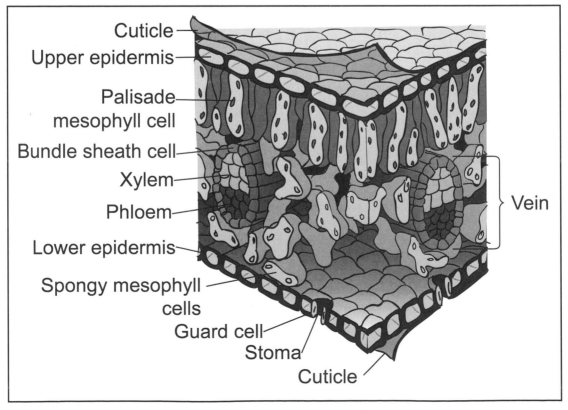

Cuticle
Upper epidermis
Palisade mesophyll cell
Bundle sheath cell
Xylem
Phloem
Lower epidermis
Spongy mesophyll cells
Guard cell
Stoma
Cuticle
Vein

1. For each statement, circle T for true and F for false. If the statement is false, replace the **bold word(s)** to make the statement true. Then write "D" for diagram or the number of the sentence(s) that best supports the answer.

    a. T F **All** plants store a large amount of food in their roots. _____

    _____

    b. T F Photosynthesis takes place mainly on **dark nights**. _____, _____

    _____

    c. T F The xylem and phloem are located on the **outer** area of the leaf. _____

    _____

    d. T F In order to make its own food, a plant needs water, sunlight, and a **gas** called carbon dioxide. _____, _____

    _____

2. What is the function of the guard cells?
    a. to keep insects off the leaf
    b. to surround the stoma so water cannot escape
    c. to open and close the stoma
    d. to make the plant green

Write the numbers of the two sentences that best support the answer. _____, _____

3. What does the word **majority** most likely mean in paragraph D?
    a. lesser part
    b. small part
    c. round part
    d. greater part

4. When looking at a leaf on a plant, what are the two top layers we are able to see?

_____

_____

5. What facts do you know about the coloring of plants?

_____

_____

Write the number of the sentence that best supports the answer. _____

6. Identify the plant part or job description as you complete the table below.

Plant Part	**Job Description**
leaf	
	support the plant
root	
	transport water and minerals
phloem	

Plants are often able to produce more food than needed on sunny days. The plant will store this extra glucose in the form of other sugars and starch. Then, when it comes time to use this stored food, the plant cells break down the glucose with the help of oxygen. This process, known as cellular respiration, produces carbon dioxide, water, and energy. This process is basically the reverse of photosynthesis, which produces glucose and oxygen.

7. Fill in the formulas for these two processes. Keep in mind that the arrow stands for "produces".

Photosynthesis:

_____ + _____ + _____ → _____ + _____

Cellular Respiration:

_____ + _____ → _____ + _____ + _____

Written Response Questions

For the following two questions, apply all of the information you have learned when answering.

8. Consider everything you have learned about the leaf of a plant as you make two or more inferences about the cuticle.

_____

_____

_____

_____

_____

_____

_____

_____

_____

_____

_____

_____

9. Explain some problems that could impact (or affect) the process of photosynthesis.

_____

_____

_____

_____

_____

_____

_____

_____

_____

_____

_____

_____

_____

30. Reproduction in Plants

A [1]Plants reproduce in more than one way. [2]Some plants need two parents to reproduce an offspring, which is known as **sexual reproduction**. [3]Other plants produce offspring with only one parent, which is called **asexual reproduction**. [4]One example of asexual reproduction is when spores released from a moss plant grow into new moss plants.

B [5]**Angiosperms** and **gymnosperms** are the two groups of vascular plants that bear seeds for reproduction. [6]Angiosperms produce seeds in flowers and include fruit trees, flowering plants such as roses and oak trees, and many more. [7]**Pollination** is the transfer of pollen grains containing **sperm** (male cells) from the **anther** to the **stigma**, which contains the **ovule** (female cell). [8]The transfer of pollen is caused by wind, water, or animals, such as birds, bats, and insects. [9]As these animals, known as **pollinators**, collect nectar from the flowers, pollen clings to them and may be dropped off at another flower. [10]When pollen from the anther is transferred to the stigma of the same flower, this is called **self-pollination**. [11]If pollen is carried from the anther of one flower to the stigma of another flower, this is called **cross-pollination**. [12]The joining of sperm and the ovule in the stigma is called **fertilization**. [13]The fertilized egg divides many times and grows to become a seed. [14]As you can see in the diagram of the apple blossom, the fruit is the result of the ovary growing around the fertilized seeds.

C [15]Gymnosperm plants usually produce their seeds in cone-like structures. [16]Scotch pines and Douglas fir trees are examples of gymnosperm plants. [17]Pollen cones are male cones that spread pollen to the female cone, usually by the wind. [18]The sperm in the pollen fertilizes the egg cells in the ovule of the female cone, causing seeds to grow within the female cone. [19]Once the seeds are fully developed, they are released from the cone.

Sexual Propagation: fruit and seed development

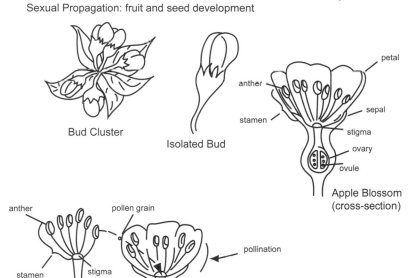

D [20]The seeds may fall directly from the parent plant to the ground or travel a long way before they are ready to grow. [21]The process by which seeds scatter from one place to another is called **dissemination**. [22]Many seeds are spread by wind or water. [23]**Hitchhiker** seeds are bristly and cling to animals' fur until they eventually fall off. [24]If seeds are inside fruit, animals may eat the fruit around the seed, leaving the seed on the ground. [25]Sometimes the animal eats the whole fruit, including the seeds. [26]Once these seeds travel through the animal's digestive system, they are released and left behind on the ground.

E [27]Inside all seeds is a tiny new plant called the **embryo**. [28]The seed protects the embryo until the conditions in the environment are right for growth. [29]The seed will then sprout and grow into a new plant. [30]As this plant grows and matures, it will repeat the life cycle of the plant.

1. For each statement, circle T for true and F for false. If the statement is false, replace the **bold word(s)** to make the statement true. Then write the number of the sentence(s) that best supports the answer.

   a. T   F   Asexual reproduction requires **two parent plants** to produce offspring. _____

   _____

   b. T   F   Pollen can travel from one plant to another in **many ways**. _____

   _____

   c. T   F   The **anther** holds female cells. _____

   _____

   d. T   F   If an apple blossom growing on an apple tree **is not fertilized**, it will then become an apple. _____

   _____

2. In paragraph A, the word **offspring** most likely means:
   a. hyper seed
   b. seasonal seed
   c. young
   d. several flowers

3. In paragraph B, the word **bear** is most likely a <u>synonym</u> of:
   a. fruit-eating animal
   b. tolerate
   c. break apart
   d. generate

4. Name the two processes in plant reproduction in which animals often assist.

   _____

   _____

   Write the numbers of the two sentences that best support the answer. _____, _____

5. Referring to the diagram in the lesson, describe how the flower changes after pollination and fertilization have taken place.

   _____

   _____

   _____

   _____

6. Fill in the table to explain how these four parts of nature can help seeds to disperse in different ways.

Dissemination		
raccoon	→	
bear	→	
wind	→	
water	→	

7. What type of environmental conditions do you think would be ideal for the embryo in a seed to grow?

   _____

   _____

   _____

8. Fill in the blanks:

   Butterflies are attracted to a flower's aroma and colorful petals. As the butterflies drink the

   _____

   in the flower,

   _____

   rubs off of the

   _____

   and clings to the butterfly.

   Write the numbers of the sentence that best supports the answer. _____

Written Response Questions

For the following two questions, apply all of the information you have learned when answering.

9. Compare and contrast the fertilization in angiosperm plants to the fertilization in gymnosperm plants.

_____

_____

_____

_____

_____

_____

_____

_____

_____

_____

_____

_____

_____

10. Macey is disappointed because her fruit plants are not producing fruit. She keeps the plants in her bedroom near a sunny window and waters them the right amount. What would you recommend to Macey to help her plants produce fruit? Why?

_____

_____

_____

_____

_____

_____

_____

_____

_____

_____

_____

_____

31. Invertebrates

A [1]The animal kingdom is divided into two major groups: **vertebrates** and **invertebrates**. [2]Vertebrate means "with a backbone." [3]Many animals, such as birds, fish, reptiles, amphibians, and mammals, are in the vertebrate group. [4]However, there are far more invertebrate (without backbone) animals on Earth. [5]View the graph below to see how the proportion of invertebrates compares to the proportion of other living organisms.

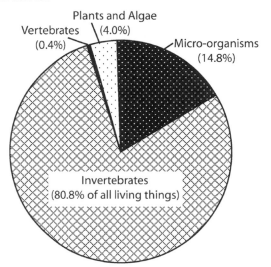

Plants and Algae (4.0%)
Vertebrates (0.4%)
Micro-organisms (14.8%)
Invertebrates (80.8% of all living things)

B [6]Some invertebrates live on land and others live in water. [7]When you walk outside in the yard or in a park, what type of animal are you most likely to see? [8]You would probably see ants on the ground and bees, flies, and butterflies on plants or flying in the air. [9]Insects are the largest part of the **Arthropod** phyla, which is the largest group of invertebrates. [10]Arthropods can be found almost everywhere, including forests, deserts, oceans, lakes, the sky, underground, and even in our homes.

C [11]Insects and other arthropods are supported by their **exoskeleton**, which also protects them like a coat of armor. [12]The word *insect* in Latin and Greek means "cut into sections." [13]The insect's body has three sections. [14]The **head** has a pair of antennae, eyes, and a mouth. [15]The **thorax**, which is the middle section, has the six legs and wings (in some species). [16]In the rear is the **abdomen**, which contains many body systems, such as the respiratory, digestive, and reproductive systems.

D [17]Insects go through a **metamorphosis**, which means that they undergo drastic changes during their life cycle. [18]To develop and grow, an insect must molt. [19]Since the exoskeleton cannot grow, the insect **molts**, or sheds this outer covering, and then grows a larger exoskeleton. [20]Some insects go through an **incomplete metamorphosis** with only three stages, such as the grasshopper. [21]After hatching from an egg, the young are called **nymphs** and look very similar to the adult. [22]As they molt and develop, they become adults. [23]Some insects go through a **complete metamorphosis** with four stages. [24]The egg is the first stage. [25]Next, the **larva** hatches from the egg. [26]During this worm-like stage, the larva looks very different from the adult. [27]Third is the **pupa** stage. [28]For this part of the metamorphosis, the larva has sealed itself into a cocoon structure. [29]During the pupa stage, the insect transforms and then finally emerges as an adult.

E [30]There are a wide variety of invertebrates on Earth beyond insects and other arthropods. [31]Study the table below to learn more about many invertebrate phyla.

Phyla	**Characteristics**	**Common Examples**
Arthropods	exoskeleton (hard outer skeleton), segmented, jointed	beetles, centipedes, spiders, shrimp, crabs
Echinoderms	marine, spiny skin	sand dollar, sea star, sea urchins
Cnidarians	aquatic, stinging cells, single opening	jellyfish, anemone, coral
Mollusks	soft body, most have shells	snails, clams, octopus, squid
Annelids	segmented worms, moist or wet environment	earthworms, leeches
Nematodes	thread-like, cylinder shaped	roundworms

1. For each statement, circle T for true and F for false. If the statement is false, replace the **bold word(s)** to make the statement true. Then write "D" for diagram or the number of the sentence(s) that best supports the answer.

   a. T F A **small** percentage of living organisms are invertebrates. _____

   _____

   b. T F Invertebrate animals **do not have** a backbone. _____

   _____

   c. T F Echinoderms are commonly found in **your yard**. _____

   _____

   d. T F The majority of people see arthropods **almost every day**. _____

   _____

2. The prefix **exo-** in the word exoskeleton most likely means:
   a. internal
   b. exit
   c. without
   d. external

3. Choose the best answer about insects. All insects:
   a. go through metamorphosis.
   b. go through the pupa stage.
   c. have three body sections.
   d. both a and c are correct.

   Write the numbers of the two sentences that best support the answer. _____, _____

4. What percent of living organisms are NOT invertebrates?

   _____

5. List the three stages an insect goes through during incomplete metamorphosis:

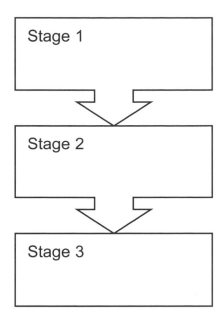

6. List the four stages an insect goes through during complete metamorphosis:

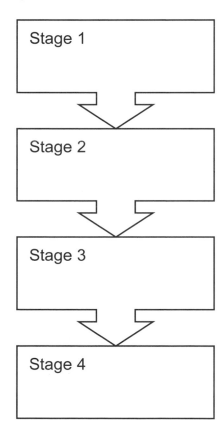

7. During one of the stages of complete metamorphosis, the insect does not eat. Which stage is this? Why?

   _____

   _____

   _____

8. Label the three sections of the insect below. Then draw and label all of the body parts from paragraph C.

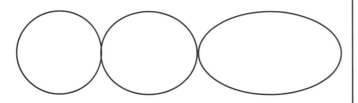

Written Response Questions

For the following two questions, apply all of the information you have learned when answering.

9. Name at least two arthropods that you have seen recently but are not named in this lesson. Explain how you know these animals are arthropods, giving at least three supporting details.

_____

_____

_____

_____

_____

_____

_____

_____

10. Imagine that you explored a beach for the day and observed many invertebrate animals in their natural habitat. Name four different invertebrates that you observed. Make sure each one is part of a different phylum. Tell which phyla each animal is part of and give a brief description of each animal.

_____

_____

_____

_____

_____

_____

_____

_____

32. Vertebrates

A [1]Which phylum in the animal kingdom do we, humans, belong to? [2]The **Chordata** phylum includes all animals that have a nerve cord at one time in their life. [3]The largest sub-phylum of Chordata is **Vertebrata**. [4]All vertebrates have a backbone, also known as a **spinal column**, which protects the spinal cord. [5]All vertebrates have an **endoskeleton**, which is an internal skeleton that supports the body. [6]Most vertebrates' muscular systems include two sets of paired limbs. [7]In humans, these are our arms and legs. [8]In other animals, these can be wings or fins.

B [9]Humans are in the class of vertebrates known as **mammals**, which also includes many other animals, such as bears, monkeys, mice, and whales. [10]The characteristic that gives mammals their name is that all female mammals produce milk for their young in **mammary glands**. [11]Most mammals give birth to live young, though there are a few that lay eggs. [12]The young mammals are cared for and have a strong resemblance to their parents. [13]Mammals are **warm-blooded**, which means they maintain a constant body temperature. [14]All mammals have hair or fur on their bodies and breathe air with lungs.

C [15]Flamingos, blue jays, owls, and eagles are a few examples of the class of vertebrates known as **birds**. [16]Like mammals, birds care for their young, breathe with lungs, and are warm-blooded. [17]All birds hatch from a hard-shelled egg. [18]They all have wings, feathers, and beaks. [19]Their feathered wings give most birds the ability to fly. [20]An important **adaptation** (feature that helps with survival) is the bird's **beak**, also called a bill in some species. [21]This important structure on the bird's head is used for a variety of tasks, such as probing for food, killing prey, eating, grooming, and feeding their young. [22]Each species of birds has a unique size and shape to its beak, which is adapted to the bird's environmental needs. [23]A hummingbird's beak is long and thin for feeding on nectar deep within a flower. [24]The large, powerful, curved beak of a parrot is used to open and consume seeds.

D [25]**Reptiles** are the class of animals with dry, thick, scaly skin, which includes all species of snakes, lizards, turtles, crocodiles, and more. [26]Even though some reptiles live on land and others in water, most reptiles lay eggs with a soft leathery shell on dry land. [27]Like birds and mammals, reptiles breathe with lungs. [28]In contrast, reptiles are **cold-blooded**. [29]This means they do not generate enough heat to keep their body temperature constant. [30]Therefore, the reptile's body temperature is usually similar to the temperature of its surroundings.

E [31]**Amphibians**, such as frogs, toads, and salamanders, are another class of vertebrate that are cold-blooded. [32]Unlike the reptile, amphibian skin is usually smooth and moist. [33]Study the diagram of the frog's life cycle, which is typical for amphibians. [34]Notice how frogs breathe through gills early in life and then develop lungs for living on land.

LIFE CYCLE OF A FROG

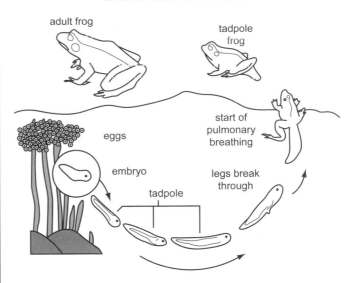

F [35]**Fish** are cold-blooded vertebrates that live in water and breathe through gills. [36]Fish have fins and are covered in scales. [37]Most fish lay eggs. [38]Some fish, such as sharks, rays, and skates, belong in a group called **cartilaginous**, also known as soft-boned fish. [39]The skeletons of these fish are made of a tissue called **cartilage** instead of hard bones. [40]Some common types of bony fish are salmon, tuna, herring, and marlin.

1. For each statement, circle T for true and F for false. If the statement is false, replace the **bold word(s)** to make the statement true. Then write "D" for diagram or the number of the sentence(s) that best supports the answer.

   a. T   F   **Endoskeleton** means to have the skeleton inside the body. _____

     _____

   b. T   F   If an animal is cold-blooded, then its body temperature **is always cold**. _____

     _____

   c. T   F   Mammals and birds are both **warm-blooded**. _____

     _____

   d. T   F   During the life cycle of the frog, the back legs grow **before** the front legs. _____

     _____

2. In paragraph C, the word **probing** most likely means:
   a. resting
   b. flying
   c. throwing
   d. searching

3. In paragraph D, the word **generate** most likely means:
   a. use
   b. create
   c. save
   d. lose

4. Mammals are different from other vertebrate animals because the females have mammary glands. How are these glands beneficial?

_____

Write the number of the sentence that best supports the answer. _____

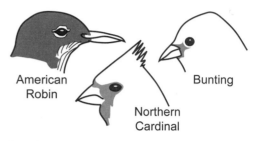

American Robin   Bunting   Northern Cardinal

5. Grosbeak birds have bills that are modified for cracking seeds. Determine which two birds above are grosbeaks. Explain your reason for choosing these two.

_____

_____

_____

_____

6. One of the birds above has a bill that is referred to as a "tweezer" beak, which is used for pulling worms out of the ground. Determine which bird this describes and explain your reasoning.

_____

_____

_____

7. Using the double Venn diagram, compare and contrast mammals and birds. List at least three characteristics in each section.

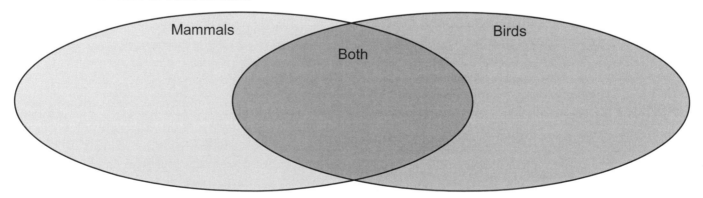

Mammals   Both   Birds

8. Using the triple Venn diagram, compare and contrast reptiles, amphibians, and fish.

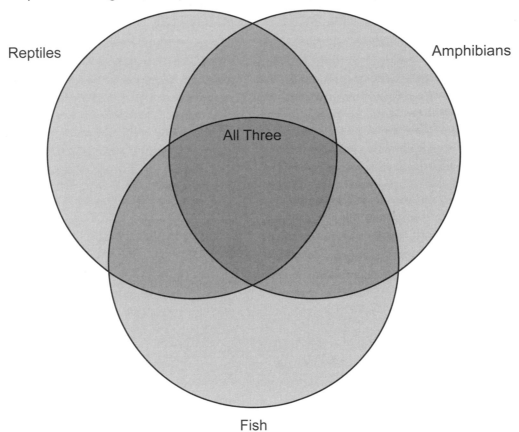

Written Response Question

For the following question, apply all of the information you have learned when answering.

9. Explain how some amphibians adapt the way they breathe to their surroundings throughout their life.

_____

_____

_____

_____

_____

_____

_____

_____

_____

_____

_____

33. Earth's Biomes

A [1]Climates vary throughout the world. [2]**Climate** is the average weather conditions of a region, which is described by the average yearly precipitation and temperature. [3]Climate affects the **abiotic factors** (nonliving things) in the environment, such as water, air, sunlight, and soil. [4]**Biotic factors** (living things) depend on abiotic factors for survival. [5]Earth is divided into large land regions, called **biomes**, which have similar plants, animals, and climate. [6]Notice in the graph below how each biome is effectively characterized by the temperature and amount of precipitation.

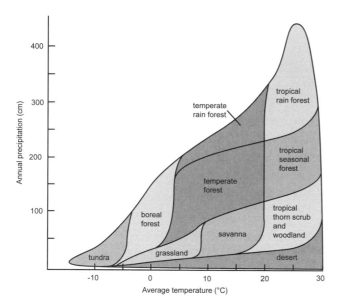

B [7]Observe the extremely low temperatures of the **tundra** biomes. [8]This severe climate causes a layer of soil to remain permanently frozen. [9]This **permafrost** layer prevents roots from growing deep in the ground; therefore, trees are quite sparse. [10]Some plants that are able to grow in the tundra's nutrient-poor soil during the short growing season are wildflowers, grasses, mosses, and dwarf shrubs. [11]Even though the precipitation is also very low, the tundra still has snowy grounds and many swamps and bogs due to the exceptionally low rate of evaporation. [12]A few of the animals that are able to live in the tundra, even with these abiotic factors, are caribou, owls, foxes, and rabbits. [13]Many of these animals have adapted to this environment by camouflaging with white coats. [14]The arctic tundra includes large areas of northern Canada and Russia.

C [15]You can determine from the graph that the **tropical rain forest** has the opposite climate of the tundra. [16]This is mainly due to their location. [17]The tropical rain forests are found in close proximity to the equator. [18]Unlike the tundra, the tropical rain forest has a very high rainfall and very hot temperatures, which is why it is home to two-thirds of all animals and plant species on Earth.

D [19]The **desert** biome is characterized by a very dry climate. [20]Unlike the tundra, the desert can lose more moisture than it receives. [21]Temperatures can be extreme due to this low moisture, changing from a daytime temperature of 50 degrees Celsius (122 degrees Fahrenheit) to a nighttime temperature of zero degrees Celsius (32 degrees Fahrenheit). [22]There are also some deserts that are cold most of the time. [23]Deserts occupy about one-third of our planet's land surface and are found on every continent. [24]The soils in most deserts have a low amount of organic materials and are usually very sandy or rocky. [25]Any organism that lives in the deserts has been able to adapt to the arid conditions. [26]To avoid moisture loss, many of the desert animals rest during the daylight hours and are awake at night, which is called being **nocturnal**. [27]Some desert animals are snakes, lizards, rodents, a few insects, and birds. [28]The sparse plant life may include shrubs, cacti, and grass that grows in bunches.

E [29]The **temperate forests** are located between the polar zones and the tropical zones (near the equator). [30]The climate in the temperate zones on Earth is subtler, with warm and cool weather changing with the seasons. [31]Biomes that lie within the temperate zones are coniferous forests, deciduous forests, and grasslands. [32]A wide range of plants and animals live within these temperate areas, including the majority of the human population.

1. For each statement, circle T for true and F for false. If the statement is false, replace the **bold word(s)** to make the statement true. Then write the number of the sentence(s) that best supports the answer.

   a. T   F   There **are not many** deserts on Earth. _____

   _____

   b. T   F   **Not many trees** grow in the tundra. _____

   _____

   c. T   F   **Not many trees** grow in the temperate forests. _____, _____

   _____

   d. T   F   The desert biome daytime temperature is **similar to** the nighttime temperature. _____

   _____

2. In paragraph D, the word **arid** most likely means:
   a. very dry
   b. moist
   c. rainy
   d. sunny

3. In paragraph E, an <u>antonym</u> for the word **subtle** is most likely:
   a. slight
   b. moist
   c. calm
   d. obvious

4. How have desert animals adapted to the dry climate?

   _____

   _____

   Write the number of the sentence that best supports the answer. _____

5. Using the graph, list the three biomes that have average temperatures that reach below zero degrees Celsius.

   _____

   _____

   _____

6. Using the graph, describe the climate in the savanna.

   _____

   _____

   _____

7. View the world map on the following page as you complete the following questions.
   a. Describe the location of the tropical rain forests of the world.

   _____

   b. How does the location affect the climate of the rain forests?

   _____

8. On the world map, label the approximate locations of the temperate forest biomes and the tundra biomes.

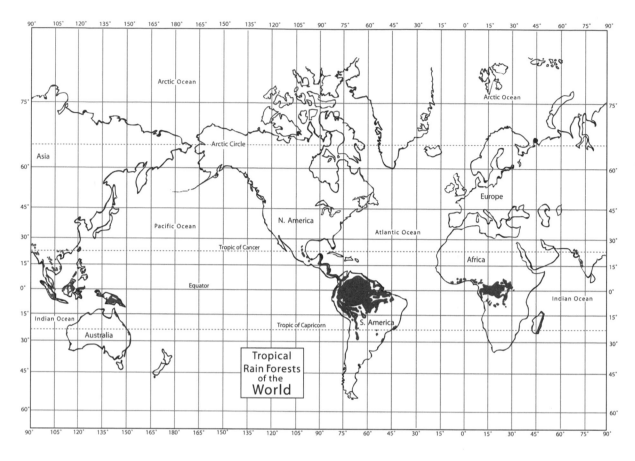

Written Response Questions

For the following two questions, apply all of the information you have learned when answering.

9. Explain how the soil in the tundra and desert are similar. How does this type of soil affect these biomes?

_____

_____

_____

_____

_____

10. Describe the type of biome where you live. Describe the climate and how it affects the abiotic factors. Then give details on how the biotic factors depend on the abiotic factors.

_____

_____

_____

_____

_____

34. Ecosystems

A [1]Earth has a huge variety of ecosystems. [2]Water ecosystems can be found in rivers, lakes, ponds, marshes, coral reefs, the deep sea, and elsewhere. [3]Land ecosystems are in forests, grasslands, deserts, and numerous other places. [4]Each ecosystem depends on the balance and interaction of the abiotic and biotic factors.

B [5]If you sat quietly beside a lake, what do you suppose you would observe? [6]Perhaps you'd see fish jumping in the water, ducks swimming by, and the breeze causing ripples in the water. [7]All of these features are part of this freshwater ecosystem. [8]An **ecosystem** is the interlinking of all living (biotic) and nonliving (abiotic) things in an area. [9]The abiotic factors of a lake ecosystem would be rocks, the lake water, rain, wind, the sunshine, the ground soil surrounding the lake, the muddy lakebed, and all other nonliving things that make up the physical surroundings. [10]The biotic things are organisms such as animals, plants, bacteria, etc.

C [11]A group of organisms of one species living in the same area is called a **population**. [12]A group of ducks, a group of bass, or millions of microscopic bacteria each make up a separate population. [13]All of the populations of organisms in an area are called a **community**. [14]Each organism has an important function within the ecosystem. [15]A **niche** is the role each species has in an ecosystem. [16]This role takes into account what an animal eats, who eats it, where it lives, and more. [17]The dragonfly's niche in a freshwater ecosystem is to fly over the surface of the water, to eat flies and mosquitoes, and to be eaten by predators, such as frogs and birds. [18]Each species has its own unique role, meaning it cannot have exactly the same niche as another species.

D [19]The feeding relationships between organisms in an ecosystem are known as both **food chains** and **food webs**. [20]The first link in the food chain is a **producer**, which is a plant, protist, or other organism that make its own food through the process of photosynthesis. [21]The second link is considered the primary **consumer**, which cannot make its own food, so it eats the producer for its energy. [22]This consumer could be an **herbivore** (plant eater) or an **omnivore** (plant and animal eater). [23]All consumers depend on other living things for survival. [24]The next link in the chain is the secondary consumer, which is a **carnivore** (animal eater). [25]An example food chain is shown within the food web diagram below. [26]It begins with the grass absorbing energy from the sun. [27]Next, the rabbit eats the grass for energy, and then the fox eats the rabbit for energy.

E [28]Notice how the food web diagram is a more complex networking of producers and consumers than a food chain. [29]A food web is more realistic, since most animals consume several different types of food for survival. [30]For example, the mouse will eat acorns, grasses, seeds, and other types of food from plants when they are available, which depends on the season. [31]The owl will hunt for and consume insects, small mammals, and even other birds.

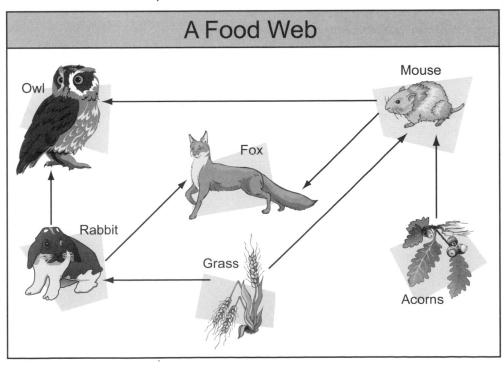

A Food Web

Owl

Mouse

Fox

Rabbit

Grass

Acorns

1. For each statement, circle T for true and F for false. If the statement is false, replace the **bold word(s)** to make the statement true. Then write the number of the sentence(s) that best supports the answer.

   a. T F **All consumers** rely solely on producers for food. ____

   _____

   b. T F One population of frogs lives in **many ponds**. ____

   _____

   c. T F The owl in the food web diagram is a **secondary consumer**. ____

   _____

   d. T F The rabbit in the food web diagram is **an omnivore**. ____

   _____

2. In paragraph B, the word **interlinking** most likely means:
   a. consuming
   b. connecting
   c. separating
   d. dividing

3. In paragraph E, an <u>antonym</u> for the word **complex** is:
   a. complicated
   b. narrow
   c. simple
   d. difficult

4. Describe the niche of an animal not mentioned in this lesson.

   Animal: _____

   Niche: _____

   _____

   _____

5. Why couldn't a food web consist of only producers?

   _____

   _____

   _____

   Write the numbers of the two sentences that best support the answer. ____, ____

6. List several biotic factors in a forest.

   _____

   _____

   _____

   _____

   _____

   _____

7. Add a picture of the sun to the food web diagram. Draw arrows to the two links that use the sun's energy to make food.

8. People are said to be "at the top of the food chain." Draw a diagram of a food chain. Begin with the sun and end with a human as a secondary consumer. Label all parts in detail.

9. Draw the same food chain again, and then add more producers and consumers to change it into a food web.

Written Response Question

For the following question, apply all of the information you have learned when answering.

10. Create an ecosystem in an aquarium. Describe the abiotic and biotic factors you would include. Describe the niche of at least two different species.

_____

_____

_____

_____

_____

_____

_____

_____

_____

_____

_____

_____

_____

_____

_____

Unit III
EARTH SCIENCE

35. Plate Tectonics: Mountains, Volcanoes, and Earthquakes

A [1]Earth's entire crust, which includes the continents and ocean basins, is constantly moving. [2]Parts of the crust slowly move into, under, or away from each other. [3]The drift of the continents is so slow (about 1.5 inches per year) that it is not noticeable unless it's viewed over millions of years.

B [4]Have you ever put together a jigsaw puzzle? [5]Think of the continents as large pieces of a puzzle. [6]Do they all fit together? [7]Look closely at their coastlines.

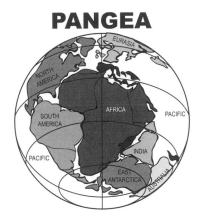

PANGEA

C [8]In 1912, Alfred Wegener, a German scientist, wrote a book called *The Origins of Continents and Oceans*, in which he explained how Earth's continents had fit together at one time as one gigantic continent. [9]He called this huge continent **Pangea**, which means "all lands." [10]His hypothesis is now known as **continental drift**.

D [11]Earth's crust and outer mantle form the **lithosphere**. [12]The lithosphere is broken into pieces called **tectonic plates**. [13]The tectonic plates float on the lower portion of Earth's mantle.

14What causes these plates to move? [15]Heat from deep in Earth's interior causes the rock in the mantle to become hotter and rise upward. [16]Then it squeezes between the edges of two plates, or **plate boundaries**. [17]This forces the plates apart. [18]This process constantly pushes the plates farther and farther apart.

E [19]Places where plates move apart are called **divergent boundaries**. [20]This type of plate movement is responsible for seafloor spreading, which is how the Mid-Atlantic Ridge and East Pacific Rise were formed.

F [21]At **convergent boundaries**, the plates are actually moving toward each other, causing a collision. [22]When there is a continent on both sides of the plates, the collision causes the crust to crumble, fold, tilt, or lift, forming mountains. [23]The Himalayan Mountains formed along a convergent boundary. [24]**Volcanoes** are also found at convergent boundaries. [25]As one plate slides under another, hot rock material in the upper mantle melts and becomes magma. [26]It can then erupt through cracks, producing volcanic mountains.

G [27]The San Andreas Fault is a famous example of a **transform fault boundary**. [28]Faults are huge cracks in Earth's crust. [29]This type of boundary occurs when plates slide past each other in different directions without moving up or down. [30]Sometimes the motion is very gradual and occasionally it is very sudden. [31]An **earthquake** is the vigorous shaking of Earth's crust due to sudden plate movements.

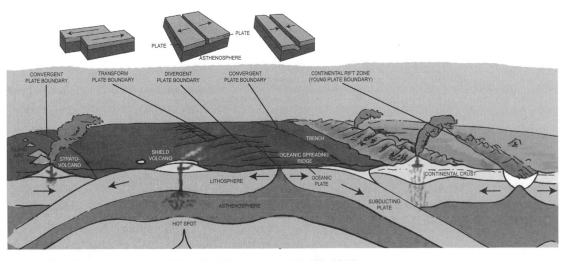

1. For each statement, circle T for true and F for false. If the statement is false, replace the **bold word(s)** to make the statement true. Then write the number of the sentence(s) that best supports the answer.

    a. T F   Earth's crust is **always** moving.
    _____

    _____

    b. T F   The tectonic plates float on the lower portion of Earth's **crust**. _____

    _____

    c. T F   **Divergent boundaries** are responsible for seafloor spreading.
    _____

    _____

    d. T F   Volcanoes are formed at **transform fault boundaries**. _____

    _____

2. The place where Earth's plates move apart is called a(n):
    a. transform fault.
    b. divergent boundary.
    c. convergent boundary.
    d. ocean plate.

    Write the number of the sentence that best supports the answer. _____

3. Most earthquakes are caused by:
    a. magma cooling on the side of a volcano.
    b. Earth's plates spreading apart.
    c. Earth's plates sliding past   each other.
    d. lava.

    Write the number of the sentence that best supports the answer. _____

4. Apply what you have read from the lesson to describe three ways that plates interact with each other.

    _____

    _____

    _____
    Write the numbers of the sentences that

best support the answer.
    _____, _____, _____

5. Refer to the lesson to explain Pangea.

    _____

    _____

    _____

    _____

    Write the numbers of the sentences that best support the answer. _____, _____

6. What are earthquakes and how are they formed?

    _____

    _____

    _____

    _____

    Write the number of the sentence that best supports the answer. _____

The Richter scale is used to measure the magnitude, or strength, of earthquakes on a scale of 1 to 10. The Mercalli scale is another system used to describe the effects of earthquakes from Type I to Type XII. The farther away a place is from the epicenter, or the surface directly above an earthquake, the less the effect will be and the lower the rating will be.

7.-8. Using the graphic on the next page, how would you compare the two scales?

    _____

    _____

    _____

    _____

    _____

    _____

Mercalli Scale

I.   Felt by almost no one

II.   Felt by very few people

III. Tremor is noticed by many people, but they often do not realize it is an earthquake.

IV.   Tremor is felt indoors by many; it feels like a truck has struck the building.

V.   Tremor is felt by nearly everyone; many people are awakened. Swaying trees and poles may be observed.

VI.   Tremor is felt by all; many people run outdoors. Furniture is moved; slight damage occurs.

VII. Everyone runs outdoors. Poorly built structures are considerably damaged; slight damage elsewhere.

VIII. Specially designed structures are damaged slightly; others collapse.

IX.   All buildings are considerably damaged; many shift off foundations. There are noticeable cracks in the ground.

X.   Many structures are destroyed. The ground is badly cracked.

XI.   Almost all structures fall. Bridges are wrecked. There are very wide cracks in the ground.

XII. There is total destruction. Waves are seen on ground. Large objects are tumbled and tossed.

Richter Scale

2.5   Tremor is generally not felt but is recorded on seismometers.

3.5   Felt by many people

4.5   Some local damage may occur.

6.0   A destructive earthquake

7.0   A major earthquake

8.0 and up   Great earthquake

Written Response Questions

For the following questions, apply all of the information you have learned when answering.

9. Why might waves from the same earthquake cause more damage in one area than another?

_____

_____

_____

_____

_____

_____

10. How are the formation of volcanoes and plate boundaries related?

_____

_____

_____

_____

_____

36. Rock Cycle, Erosion, and Deposition

A   [1]Where do rocks come from? [2]Simple! [3]All rocks come from other rocks. [4]Rocks are constantly changing into other rocks in a never-ending cycle called the **rock cycle**. [5]The diagram below shows the different ways that one type of rock can become another rock.

B   [6]As you can see, weathering, erosion, and deposition play important roles in the creation of rocks and landforms. [7]**Weathering** is the process of breaking down rock into soil, sand, and other sediment by wind, rain, snow, sleet, or hail. [8]After weathering has broken down the rock into sediment, erosion or deposition may occur. [9]**Erosion** is a process in which Earth's surface is worn away by wind and water. [10]**Deposition** is a process in which sediment is dropped or deposited to a new location.

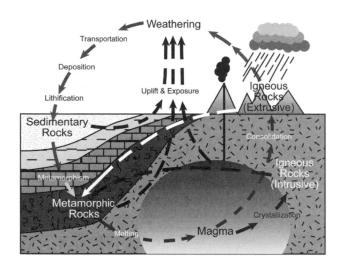

[11]There are three main types of rocks: igneous, sedimentary, and metamorphic. [12]Each type of rock is formed in a unique way that takes more than a million years.

C   [13]**Igneous rocks** form when rock minerals are melted, cooled, and become solid again. [14]There are many kinds of igneous rocks. [15]Their differences depend on where the rock was formed. [16]**Intrusive rocks** form below Earth's surface when the magma within Earth cools and hardens. [17]These rocks appear after the rocks above them have been worn away by weathering or erosion. [18]**Extrusive rocks** form when the lava above the surface of Earth cools and hardens. [19]Granite, basalt, obsidian, and pumice are just a few examples of igneous rocks.

D   [20]**Sedimentary rocks** are formed from eroded layers of sediment materials, such as deceased plants and animals and pieces of rocks, which settle in layers on top of each other and harden over time. [21]Fossils are most often found in layers of sedimentary rock.   [22]Some examples of sedimentary rock are rock salt, halite, limestone, sandstone, and shale. [23]**Conglomerates** are sedimentary rocks that are made up of pebbles, boulders, or shells that become hardened together in clumps.

E   [24]A **metamorphic rock** was once another type of rock that was "changed" over time. [25]It may have been an igneous, sedimentary, or even a metamorphic rock that changed through extreme heat and pressure. [26]Metamorphic rocks usually form deep below Earth's surface.   [27]Once a metamorphic rock forms, it does not melt; its structure and texture change instead. [28]Gneiss, quartzite, slate, and marble are a few examples of metamorphic rocks.

1. For each statement, circle T for true and F for false. If the statement is false, replace the **bold word(s)** to make the statement true. Then write the number of the sentence(s) that best supports the answer.

   a. T F **Erosion** is the process of breaking down rock into soil, sand, and other sediment by wind, rain, snow, sleet, or hail. _____

      _____

   b. T F The process in which sediment is dropped or deposited to a new location is called **deposition**. _____

      _____

   c. T F **Intrusive rocks** form when the lava above the surface of Earth cools and hardens. _____

      _____

   d. T F Rocks are always changing into other rocks in a never-ending cycle called the **rock cycle**. _____

      _____

2. The process in which Earth's surface is worn away is called:
   a. sand.
   b. conglomerates.
   c. erosion.
   d. deposition.

   Write the number of the sentence that best supports the answer. _____

3. Which is **not** an example of a metamorphic rock?
   a. gneiss
   b. granite
   c. quartzite
   d. marble

   Write the number of the sentence that best supports the answer. _____

4. Use the diagram of the rock cycle and the lesson to explain how igneous rocks are formed.

   _____
   _____
   _____
   _____

   Write the number of the sentence that best supports the answer. _____

5. Use the diagram of the rock cycle and the lesson to describe the different ways sedimentary rocks form.

   _____
   _____
   _____
   _____

   Write the numbers of the sentences that best support the answer. _____, _____

6. Use the diagram of the rock cycle and the lesson to explain the process that changes rock into metamorphic rock.

   _____
   _____
   _____
   _____

   Write the numbers of the sentences that best support the answer.

   _____, _____, _____

Scientists use two ways to try to determine the relative age of rocks. One way is superposition, which means that in a column of rock layers, the bottom layer is the oldest and the top layer is the youngest. The other way is called original horizontality, which explains that sedimentary rocks form in horizontal layers.

The discovery of radioactivity has also helped scientists determine the age of a rock. They can do this by measuring the time is takes for half the mass of a radioactive element in a rock to break apart, or decay, into a new product. This happens at a rate called half-life. Scientists then compare the amount of the original element to the amount of the decay product. This will give the scientists the absolute age of a rock.

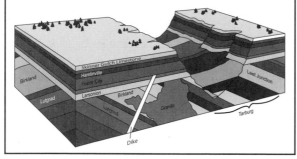

8. Complete and explain this half-life model table.

Number of atoms	60 atoms	30 atoms	15 atoms
	40 atoms	20 atoms	
	0	1	2

Half-life intervals

7. What determines a scientist's ability to tell relative age?

_____

_____

_____

_____

_____

_____

_____

_____

Written Response Questions

For the following two questions, apply all of the information you have learned when answering.

9. How do scientists believe fossils help them tell the age of a rock?

_____

_____

_____

_____

10. Metamorphic and igneous rocks form from heat. Why are they different?

_____

_____

_____

_____

37. Properties of Rocks and Minerals

A ¹How would you distinguish one mineral from another? ²A **mineral** is a naturally occurring solid with a definite structure and composition. ³There are specific **physical properties** that scientists use to identify rocks or minerals. ⁴These properties are color, hardness, streak, transparency, luster, cleavage, fracture, specific gravity, and crystal form or structure. ⁵A mineral's properties are determined by the way it is formed.

B ⁶A **rock** can be one mineral or a mixture of minerals. ⁷Since rocks are more often mixtures of minerals, it is not always easy to tell them apart. ⁸One way to tell rocks apart is by the minerals they contain. ⁹For example, **granite** is made up of the minerals feldspar, mica, hornblende, and quartz.

C ¹⁰**Color** is usually the first property we notice when identifying rocks. ¹¹Some minerals are always one color, which makes them easy to identify. ¹²For example, malachite is always green. ¹³However, some rocks can be chemically changed in a way that alters their color, like quartz. ¹⁴In its purest form it is clear, but with traces of iron quartz becomes purple and is called amethyst.

D ¹⁵The Mohs' Hardness Scale, shown in the diagram, identifies hardness in rocks. ¹⁶A way to test the hardness is to scratch one mineral with another. ¹⁷A harder mineral will scratch a softer mineral. ¹⁸Friedrich Mohs, a German mineralogist, used this fact in 1822 to create a scale of hardness. ¹⁹It is called the Mohs' Hardness Scale and ranks ten minerals from softest to hardest. ²⁰The number one represents the softest mineral, and number ten represents the hardest.

Mineral Hardness

Mohs' Hardness Scale		Approximate Hardness of Common Objects
Talc	1	
Gypsum	2	Fingernail (2.5)
Calette	3	Copper Penny (3.5)
Fluorite	4	Iron Nail (4.5)
Apatite	5	Glass (5.5)
Feldspar	6	Steel File (6.5)
Quartz	7	Streak Plate (7.0)
Topaz	8	
Corundum	9	
Diamond	10	

E ²¹The **streak** of a mineral is its color when it's rubbed across an unglazed tile of white porcelain. ²²The streak may also be found by grinding the mineral into a powder. ²³It's interesting to know that quartz will leave a white streak whether it's a purple amethyst, a pink rose quartz, or a brown smoky quartz.

F ²⁴The property of **transparency** describes how well light passes through a mineral. ²⁵There are three categories of transparency: transparent, translucent, and opaque. ²⁶It is possible to see through **transparent** minerals. ²⁷Some light can pass through **translucent** minerals, but you cannot see through them. ²⁸No light can pass through an **opaque** mineral.

G ²⁹Another property is **luster**, which is how a mineral reflects light. ³⁰It may be shiny, dull, silky, or glassy. ³¹Luster should be observed on a freshly cut piece of rock.

H ³²**Cleavage** or **fracture** of a mineral is identified by the way it breaks. ³³It may break in two or more directions. ³⁴Some common forms are **cubic**, **rhombohedral** (six-sided prism), and **basal** (along a plane parallel to the base of the mineral) **cleavages**. ³⁵Not all minerals cleave easily. ³⁶Some may fracture. ³⁷Some common types of fractures are **conchoidal** (a "shell-like" fracture with a smooth, curved surface); fibrous, or splintery; rough or jagged; and uneven, or irregular.

I ³⁸**Specific gravity** is a measure of the density of a mineral. ³⁹Some minerals are heavier than others even if they are the same size.

J ⁴⁰Another way to distinguish minerals is by their **structure** or **crystal form**. ⁴¹This is the way the molecules of the rock fit together. ⁴²It may be one of six crystal system forms, or it may appear to be made of large pieces or sections stuck together.

K ⁴³A very useful tool to have when identifying rocks is a rock field guide. ⁴⁴This will help you compare the physical properties of various rocks and minerals.

1. For each statement, circle T for true and F for false. If the statement is false, replace the **bold word(s)** to make the statement true. Then write the number of the sentence(s) that best supports the answer.
   a. T F   Rocks **can** be minerals. ____

   _____

   b. T F   The Mohs' Scale identifies **minerals** in rocks. ____

   _____

   c. T F   No light can pass through **translucent** minerals. ____

   _____

   d. T F   Specific gravity is the **volume** of a mineral. ____

   _____

2. What is the best definition of the word **cleave** as it is used in paragraph H?
   a. split
   b. penetrate
   c. accomplish
   d. to be faithful

3. Refer to the diagram in the lesson to name the softest and hardest minerals, respectfully.
   a. mica and granite
   b. quartz and glass
   c. copper and fingernail
   d. talc and diamond

4. Apply what you have learned from the lesson to list at least three properties of rocks.

   _____

   _____

   _____

   Write the number of the sentence that best supports the answer.

   ____

5. Based on what you have read from the lesson, explain Mohs' Hardness Scale and its purpose.

   _____

   _____

   _____

   Write the numbers of the sentences that best support the answer.
   ____, ____, ____

6. Refer back to the lesson and list at least four minerals.

   _____

   _____

   _____

   Write the numbers of the sentences that best support the answer. ___, ___, ___

   ┌─────────────────────────────────────┐
   Gemstones are minerals or rocks that can be cut and polished to use as jewelry or other ornaments. A precious gemstone is beautiful, durable, and rare compared to a semiprecious gemstone, which may have only one or two of these qualities.
   └─────────────────────────────────────┘

7. Apply what you have read in the lesson to explain how you would distinguish a genuine diamond from a fake.

   _____

   _____

   _____

   _____

   _____

The Importance of Rocks and Minerals		
Name	Type of Rock	Use
Basalt	Igneous	Used in road building materials
Calcite	Mineral	Used in cements and mortars and the production of lime
Granite	Igneous	Used for buildings, monuments, and tombstones
Marble	Metamorphic	Used in buildings, floors, and tile in bathrooms
Obsidian	Igneous	Used in making arrowheads and knives
Pumice	Igneous	Used in scouring, scrubbing, and polishing materials
Quartz	Mineral	Used in making glass, electrical components, and optical lenses
Sandstone	Sedimentary	Used in the building industry for houses
Slate	Metamorphic	Used for roofs, chalkboards, and patio walks

8. Use the information from the chart to support the statement, "minerals are important in our life."

_____

_____

_____

_____

_____

_____

Written Response Questions

For the following two questions, apply all of the information you have learned when answering.

9. What characteristic of minerals does the property of transparency describe?

_____

_____

_____

_____

_____

_____

_____

10. Suppose you have a mineral whose hardness is unknown. Explain how you would determine its hardness using the Mohs' Hardness Scale.

_____

_____

_____

_____

_____

_____

_____

_____

38. Geological Time

A [1]How old is Earth? [2]Most scientists believe the history of Earth can be found in its rock layers. [3]There are two ideas scientists use for finding the age of rocks. [4]One is **original horizontality**, which is the idea that many kinds of rocks form flat, horizontal layers. [5]The other idea is **superposition**, which is the idea that in a sequence of rock layers, the bottom layer is the oldest and the top layer is the youngest.

B [6]British geologist Arthur Holmes developed the first **geological time scale** in 1913. [7]He used radioactivity to try to identify the age of Earth, which he estimated to be about four billion years old.

C [8]**Geological time** is a scale used by geologists to measure Earth's development. [9]This theory is made up of four **eons**, which are the largest divisions, spanning many hundreds of millions of years. [10]The eons are broken down into four **eras**. [11]Each era is identified by the kinds of life on Earth, designated by fossils from that time. [12]The eras are then broken down even further into **periods**, which lasted from two million to eighty million years. [13]During each period, major changes occurred on Earth's crust. [14]The periods are further broken down into **epochs** and **ages**.

D [15]What was Earth like in its earliest eras? [16]Most geologists believe it began with the **Precambrian Era** that lasted about four billion years and covers the majority of Earth's history. [17]The earliest known marine fossils are believed to date back to this era. [18]Wormlike creatures called Spriggina lived on the ocean floor at the end of the Precambrian Era.

E [19]Most scientists believe the **Paleozoic Era** began when many-celled organisms quickly reproduced. [20]Fossil records during the **Cambrian Period** of that era imply that there was a large increase in the number and variety of creatures on Earth, including assorted fish and animals with shells. [21]These scientists believe that trilobites began to appear during this period. [22]It is also believed this was the time when the earliest vertebrates (animals with backbones) began to appear.

GEOLOGICAL TIME SCALE				
Time Units of the Geological Time Scale				Development of Plants and Animals
Eon	Era	Period	Epoch	
Phanerozoic	Cenozoic	Quaternary	Holocene 0.01*	Earliest Homo sapiens
			Pleistocene 1.6	
		Tertiary	Pliocene 5.3	Earliest Hominids
			Miocene 23.8	
			Oligocene 33.7	"Age of Mammals"
			Eocene 55	
			Paleocene 65	
	Mesozoic	Cretaceous 145	"Age of Reptiles"	Extinction of dinosaurs and many other species
		Jurassic 208		First flowering plants
		Triassic 248		First birds Dinosaurs dominant First mammals
	Paleozoic	Permian 286	"Age of Amphibians"	Extinction of trilobites and many other marine animals
		Carboniferous: Pennsylvanian 320		First reptiles
		Carboniferous: Mississippian 360		Large coal swamps Amphibians abundant
		Devonian 410	"Age of Fishes"	First amphibians First insect fossils
		Silurian 438		
		Ordovician 505	"Age of Invertebrates"	First land plants First fish
		Cambrian 545		Trilobites dominant First organism with shells
		Vendian 650	"Soft-bodied faunas"	Abundant Ediacaran faunas
Proterozoic		2500		First multi-celled organisms
Archean		Collectively called Precambrian 3800		
Hadean		Comprises about 87% of geological time scale		First one-celled organisms
				Age of oldest rocks
		* Numbers represent millions of years ago		Origin of Earth
		4600		

F [23]Most scientists believe the era we live in now is the **Cenozoic Era**. [24]It began about 70 million years ago. [25]As some animals and plants became extinct, new groups have appeared.

1. For each statement, circle T for true and F for false. If the statement is false, replace the **bold word(s)** to make the statement true. Then write the number of the sentence(s) that best supports the answer.

   a. T F   Earth is about four **billion** years old. _____

      _____

   b. T F On the geological time scale, **eras** are identified by fossils from that time. _____

      _____

   c. T F   The **Paleozoic Era** covers the majority of Earth's history. _____

      _____

   d. T F   We now live in the **Cambrian Period**. _____

      _____

2. The history of Earth can be found in its:
   a. minerals.
   b. rock layers.
   c. soil.
   d. particles.

   Write the number of the sentence that best supports the answer. _____

3. The earliest known marine fossils are believed to date back to the:
   a. Paleozoic Era.
   b. Cambrian Period.
   c. Precambrian Era.
   d. Cenozoic Era.

   Write the number of the sentence that best supports the answer. _____

4. Refer to the timeline and lesson to list some of the characteristics of Earth in its earliest eras.

   _____

   _____

   _____

   _____

5. Explain the difference between original horizontality and superposition.

   _____

   _____

   _____

   _____

   Write the numbers of the sentences that best support the answer. _____, _____

6. Which time period shows the most development of life? What life does it show?

   _____

   _____

   _____

   _____

   Write the numbers of the sentences that best support the answer.

   _____, _____, _____, _____

7. Based on what you have read in the lesson, what role do fossils play in the geologic time scale? Give at least three examples of fossils that scientists have identified and the time period to which they belong.

   _____

   _____

   _____

   _____

   _____

   _____

   _____

Most fossils are formed when a plant or animal dies and is buried in mud or silt. Their soft tissues decompose, leaving the bones or shells. Over time, sediment settles over the remains and hardens into rock. Sometimes the bones decay and minerals may replace the remains through a process called petrification.

8. How do fossils give scientists clues about life millions of years ago?

_____

_____

_____

_____

Written Response Questions

For the following two questions, apply all of the information you have learned when answering.

9. Explain geological time.

_____

_____

_____

_____

_____

_____

_____

_____

_____

_____

_____

10. Study the geological time scale. What does it tell you about the history of vertebrates?

_____

_____

_____

_____

_____

_____

_____

_____

_____

_____

_____

39. Natural Resources

A [1]**Natural resources** consist of any useful things from nature that people want or need, such as soil, energy, water, minerals, and plant and animal life. [2]People have been using these natural resources at a faster rate than they can be replaced. [3]Soil and minerals are considered **nonrenewable resources** because most scientists believe they take thousands of years to form and once they are used up, they are gone. [4]**Renewable resources** can be replaced as they are used. [5]**Reusable resources** are natural resources that can be used more than once if they are not polluted.

B [6]The **soil** on Earth is composed of weathered rock, water, air, bacteria, and decayed plants and animals. [7]It is considered a nonrenewable resource that people are damaging by burying garbage in landfills, planting too many crops without crop rotation, spraying the soil with chemicals, allowing farm animals to overgraze, and cutting down too many forests.

C [8]**Energy** comes in different forms, such as heat energy, light, mechanical energy, electrical energy, chemical energy, and nuclear energy. [9]People use energy to do everything from walking and cooking to putting astronauts in space. [10]Nonrenewable resources such as oil, natural gas, coal, and uranium supply people with most of their energy. [11]Most scientists believe it took millions of years to form these resources. [12]These energy sources are used to supply electricity for our homes, businesses, schools, and factories. [13]We also need gas, propane, and diesel fuel for transportation, heating, and cooking.

D [14]Some **energy** sources, such as solar energy, wind energy, geothermal energy (energy from within Earth), biomass energy (energy from plants), and hydropower (energy from water) are renewable resources. [15]We use these alternate forms of energy for heat and electricity also.

E [16]**Water** is considered a reusable resource since it can be replenished and purified through the water cycle. [17]Earth's oceans are an important resource because they supply food, minerals, fossil fuels, and water. [18]**Desalination** turns ocean water into useful fresh water by extracting salt and other materials from the seawater. [19]**Groundwater** is water that seeps into the ground from precipitation and supplies people with the majority of their fresh water.

F [20]Although water is considered a reusable resource, it can become too polluted for use. [21]Pollution is partially due to chemicals in the air and on the ground that are picked up by precipitation, causing runoffs into our lakes, rivers, and streams. [22]Factories that illegally dump waste into water also contribute to pollution.

G [23]**Forests** are considered a renewable resource only if the trees are replaced at the same rate at which they are used. [24]Trees supply the world with lumber, paper, cardboard, tar, turpentine, and food. [25]Most animals also need forests for shelter and food.

H [26]**Plants** and **animals** are valuable renewable resources that provide people with food, clothing, homes, medicine, and many other products. [27]Photosynthesis is very important for providing oxygen and filtering the air people breathe. [28]Many plants and animals are disappearing because people are destroying their habitats. [29]Today, approximately 20,000 species of birds, mammals, invertebrates, and plants are in danger of extinction.

I [30]Many governments have created and passed laws to protect our natural resources. [31]Everyone can help by saving or **conserving** these resources. [32]The three R's – reduce, reuse, and recycle – are important steps that can help conservation. [33]**Reduce** means to cut back on the use of resources. [34]Use them wisely. [35]**Reuse**, or don't throw away, items that can be used over again. [36]This saves the resources needed to make new products. [37]Finally, **recycle**, or use existing products to make other products.

1. For each statement, circle T for true and F for false. If the statement is false, replace the **bold word(s)** to make the statement true. Then write the number of the sentence(s) that best supports the answer.
   a. T F Soil is believed to be a **renewable resource** made of weathered rock, water, air, bacteria, and decayed plants and animals. _____

   _____

   b. T F You use **energy** when you walk. _____

   _____

   c. T F Most of our drinking water comes from **groundwater** that seeps into the ground from precipitation. _____

   _____

   d. T F Animals are considered a **nonrenewable resource**. _____

   _____

2. Natural resources are:
   a. useful things from nature that can be replaced.
   b. useful things from nature that are used for fuel.
   c. useful things from nature that cannot be replaced.
   d. useful things from nature that people want or need.

   Write the number of the sentence that best supports the answer. _____

3. Which of the following is **not** believed to be a renewable resource?
   a. forest
   b. water
   c. minerals
   d. plants

   Write the number of the sentence that best supports the answer. _____

4. Refer to the lesson to explain the three R's – reduce, reuse, and recycle. Give an example of each one.

   _____
   _____
   _____
   _____

   Write the numbers of the sentences that best support the answer.
   _____, _____, _____

5. Why would it be better to use alternate forms of energy for heat and electricity?

   _____
   _____
   _____
   _____

   Write the number of the sentence that best supports the answer. _____

6. After reading the lesson, what would you do differently to help conserve Earth's natural resources?

   _____
   _____
   _____
   _____

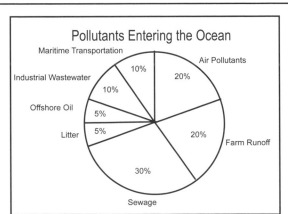

The circle graph shows many ways that Earth's water is becoming polluted.

7. What is the most common form of pollution, and where does it come from?

_____

_____

_____

_____

8. How does the way a farmer uses his or her land affect natural resources?

_____

_____

_____

_____

Write the number of the sentence that best supports the answer. _____

Written Response Questions

For the following two questions, apply all of the information you have learned when answering.

9. How would your life change if water were a nonrenewable resource?

_____

_____

_____

_____

_____

_____

_____

_____

_____

10. Use supporting details from the lesson to explain how pollution harms Earth's natural resources.

_____

_____

_____

_____

_____

_____

_____

_____

_____

40. Ocean Exploration

A [1]If you were able to view Earth from space, you would see that about 70% of it is covered by water. [2]To date, human eyes have viewed only about 1% of these vast ocean waters. [3]People have been trying to explore the oceans for thousands of years. [4]Underwater exploration is not only very difficult, it is very dangerous, as well. [5]The oceans are extremely large bodies of water that are very dark, deep, and exceptionally cold. [6]Another factor that contributes to the difficulty of exploration is that underwater pressure can exceed more than 16,000 pounds per square inch. [7]That's more pressure than you would experience if an adult elephant stood on you!

B [8]Nearly all underwater discoveries depend on **submersibles**, such as remotely operated vehicles (ROVs) and automatic underwater vehicles (AUVs). [9]Scientists also use side-scan **sonar** devices attached to ships at the ocean's surface to create maps of the seafloor.

C [10]Even with these tools, it is still difficult for **oceanographers** to study large areas of the ocean floor, so many areas have yet to be explored. [11]To assist with their studies, these scientists have relied on **satellites** in outer space that have specialized sensors to measure the topography of the ocean floor, the surface temperatures, and ocean currents.

D [12]The Atlantic Ocean, Pacific Ocean, Indian Ocean, Southern Ocean, and Arctic Ocean are the five oceans that cover Earth. [13]Deep under these waters lie large, spreading mountain ranges, active volcanoes, plateaus, and trenches.

E [14]Surrounding the edges of all oceans is an area of shallow water that may reach depths up to about 130 meters (430 feet) called the **continental shelf**. [15]The continental shelves end at areas called **continental slopes**, which lead to the deep, dark areas of the **ocean basin** that may reach depths of 2.5 to 3.5 miles. [16]Deeper into the waters is the **abyssal plain**, which is the flat ocean floor. [17]The deepest area known thus far is the Mariana Trench at 11,035 meters (36,204 feet) down. [18]It is located south of Japan. [19]Earthquakes and volcanoes also occur in the abyss. [20]The volcanoes that arise from this area may, over time, form islands.

F [21]The oceans are also home to millions of plants and animals that live in **life zones** that can be located from the surface to deep in the trenches. [22]**Phytoplanktons** are microscopic creatures that live near the surface. [23]They are the main source of food for animals that live in the different zones of the sea. [24]All plants and numerous animals live in the **sunlit zone**, which is the upper layer of the ocean where sunlight can enter and plants can make food through photosynthesis. [25]The **twilight zone** receives some light from the sun but not enough for plants to grow. [26]The **deep ocean zone** is sunless and very cold. [27]Animals in this zone mainly feed on dead plankton. [28]The **abyssal zone** is the completely dark, icy cold bottom layer of the ocean. [29]Here there are animals that produce light from their own bodies. [30]Finally, the waters that are located in the ocean's deepest trenches are in the **hadal zone**.

G [31]The variety of life in the sea provides a complex food web that allows all organisms to survive.

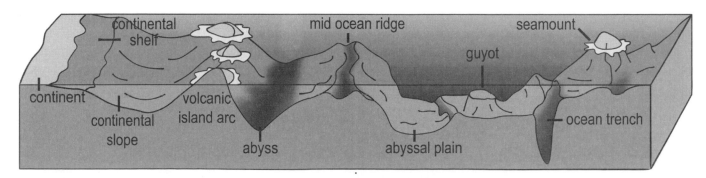

1. For each statement, circle T for true and F for false. If the statement is false, replace the **bold word(s)** to make the statement true. Then write the number of the sentence(s) that best supports the answer.

   a. T F About **three-fourths** of Earth is covered by water. _____

   _____

   b. T F Almost all underwater discoveries depend on **submersibles**. _____

   _____

   c. T F The deepest ocean area known is the **Mid-Atlantic Ridge**. _____

   _____

   d. T F Oceanographers use **sonar devices** in outer space to measure the topography of the ocean floor, the surface temperatures, and the ocean currents. _____

   _____

2. Scientists explore the oceans with:
   a. sonar devices.
   b. submersibles.
   c. satellites.
   d. all of the above.

   Write the number of the sentences that best support the answer. _____, _____, _____

3. What is the most likely meaning of the word **trenches** as it appears in paragraph F?
   a. long, steep valleys
   b. ditches
   c. type of volcanoes
   d. mountain ranges

4. From what you have read about ocean exploration, what can you infer about the importance of submersibles?

   _____

   _____

   _____

   _____

   Write the numbers of the sentences that best support the answer.

   _____, _____, _____

5. What evidence can you find from the lesson to explain why only about 1% of the waters on Earth have been explored?

   _____

   _____

   _____

   _____

   _____

   Write the numbers of the sentences that best support the answer. _____, _____

6. List four of the important discoveries that have been made by exploring the ocean waters.

   _____

   _____

   _____

   _____

   _____

   Write the numbers of the sentences that best support the answer. _____, _____

Water pressure comes from the weight of the water overhead. The weight of the water also depends on the height of the water. Earth's atmosphere exerts a force on our bodies equal to 14.7 pounds per square inch, or psi. At sea level this is known as 1 Atmosphere of Pressure, or 1 ATM.

A one-inch column of water 33 feet tall weighs 14.7 pounds. So at a depth of 33 feet, a diver experiences twice the amount of pressure. This means the diver is under a pressure of 29.4 pounds per square inch, or psi.

7. What would a diver feel at 66 feet down?

_____

_____

_____

_____

8. The ocean contains a large variety of plant and animal life. Refer to the lesson to complete the chart about the different life zones. Write a short description of the life that exists in each zone.

<u>Sea level</u>

_____

_____

_____

_____

Written Response Questions

For the following two questions, apply all of the information you have learned when answering.

9. Why do you think it's important to explore the ocean floor?

_____

_____

_____

_____

_____

_____

_____

10. If you were an oceanographer, what method would you choose to explore the ocean floor? Why?

_____

_____

_____

_____

_____

_____

41. Ocean Resources

A [1]Can you name anything that you used today that came from the ocean? [2]If you mentioned food, clothing, energy, or minerals, you're probably right! [3]The ocean is also used for travel, shipping, and recreation. [4]It contains a tremendous amount of biological and physical resources for the entire world. [5]**Biological resources** include food, chemicals secreted from living organisms, and the living organisms themselves. [6]**Physical resources** are products such as sand, salt, gravel, and the water that comes from the ocean. [7]Sometimes resources may be considered both biological and physical, such as oil and gas, because they are fossil fuels.

B [8]**Biological resources**, such as marine life, provide food, medicine, and other health products. [9]About 200 billion pounds of fish are caught each year. [10]Pharmaceutical companies are always researching ways to utilize marine bacteria, fish and plants to aid the fight against life-threatening illnesses. [11]Large kelp beds also provide a great source of the world's **algin**, which is used for its nutritional value and as a thickener in food. [12]**Agar** is also extracted from seaweed and is used in the medical field as a culture medium for testing and growing bacteria. [13]**Carrageenin**, another seaweed product, is used in lunchmeats, pet foods and toothpaste.

C [14]Many new fisheries have opened as a result of older ones becoming depleted. [15]Governments around the world have worked together to protect many species of fish so commercial fishermen don't over-fish areas.

D [16]Living organisms also provide recreational enjoyment for people who view and study marine life in aquariums. [17]Whale watching is also a recreational activity in many areas.

E [18]The oceans contain **physical resources**, such as bromine, salt, and magnesium. [19]Other minerals, such as diamonds, gold, silver, and metal ores, are very plentiful in the oceans but are more difficult to mine there than on land.

F [20]Ocean water itself is another important resource that is used to make fresh water through the desalination process. [21]Desalination plants create fresh water where it may be in short supply. [22]Ocean water is also used as a coolant in power plants or for the actual production of power.

G [23]The oceans also supply the most renewable energy resources for the world via the tides, currents, waves, and temperature differences. [24]Off-shore wind farms, turbines that use waves and currents, and ocean thermal energy conversion are just some of the newest technologies being developed to capture some of the oceans' energy.

H [25]Resources that are considered both **physical and biological** supply more than one-fifth of the world's oil and gas. [26]They are the nonrenewable fossil fuels, which most scientists believe are products of organisms that died millions of years ago but did not decompose. [27]The theory is they became compressed and changed into the petroleum products we use every day.

I [28]Humans have an important role: to determine the future availability of our ocean resources. [29]Their impact can be used to prevent ocean pollution and the destruction of habitats found in or near the ocean. [30]Look at the graph below. [31]It shows the drastic decline in New York's clam harvests from 1970-2002.

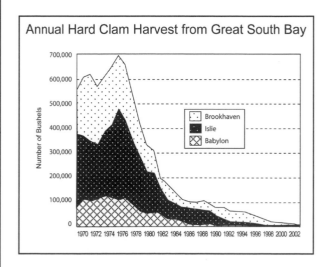

Annual Hard Clam Harvest from Great South Bay

J [32]The more we know about the huge waters of Earth, the better we can help protect these resources.

1. For each statement, circle T for true and F for false. If the statement is false, replace the **bold word(s)** to make the statement true. Then write the number of the sentence(s) that best supports the answer.

     a.   T   F   **Physical resources** include food, chemicals, and living organisms. ____

       _____

     b.   T   F   **Seaweed** is used in lunchmeats, pet food, and toothpaste. ____

       _____

     c.   T   F   Desalination plants create **table salt** because it may be in short supply in some areas. ____

       _____

     d.   T   F   Ocean resources supply more than one-fifth of the world's **oil and gas**. ____

       _____

2. In paragraph H, the word **compressed** most likely means:
     a. expanded
     b. flattened
     c. pressed together
     d. stretched

3. In paragraph H, the word **decompose** most likely means:
     a. distill
     b. separate into parts
     c. die
     d. decay

4. The ocean supplies many resources for people. Name at least three ways the ocean is considered a resource.

     _____

     _____

     _____

     _____

Write the numbers of the sentences that best support the answer.

____, ____, ____

5. Use the graph in the lesson to infer the cause of the trend that is occurring in clam harvesting in Great South Bay, from 1970 through 2002. Why do you think this is happening?

     _____

     _____

     _____

     _____

6. Complete the Venn diagram by giving examples from the lesson.

<u>Resources</u>

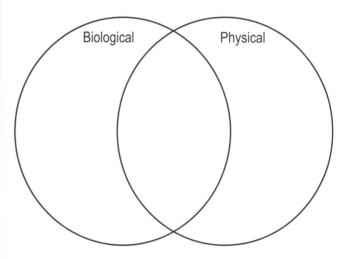

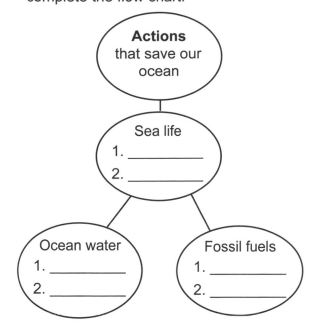

Countries that are situated along the coast have control of the sea that reaches out up to 22 kilometers from their shore.

7. What do you think nations can do to help fish stocks recover?

_____

_____

8. Name some ways Earth's water resources can be protected. Fill in the blanks to complete the flow chart.

Actions
that save our ocean

Sea life
1. _____
2. _____

Ocean water
1. _____
2. _____

Fossil fuels
1. _____
2. _____

Written Response Questions

For the following two questions, apply all of the information you have learned when answering.

9. Why are oceans important to people?

_____

_____

_____

_____

_____

_____

_____

10. Name some of the things you used today that relied on ocean resources.

_____

_____

_____

_____

_____

_____

42. Earth, Moon, and Sun

A ¹The sun, Earth, and the moon have a special relationship that causes our days, years, and seasons. ²Earth takes 365 days (one year) to move on a path, or **revolve**, around the sun. ³It is always **rotating**, or spinning, as it revolves around the sun at an average distance of 93 million miles (150 million km). ⁴The path Earth moves along is an **ellipse**, which looks like a circle that has been stretched. ⁵It takes 24 hours (one day) for Earth to rotate on its axis. ⁶The **axis** is an imaginary line that goes through Earth from the North and South poles. ⁷The part of Earth facing the sun receives light while the other side is dark, which is what gives us day and night.

B ⁸The number of hours of daylight changes during the seasons because of Earth's tilt on its axis. ⁹It rotates 15 degrees every hour, which is why time zones change by one hour. ¹⁰Earth has 24 **standard time zones** that are approximately 15 degrees wide in longitude. ¹¹The **International Date Line** is the line of longitude on the globe that is considered the location where a new day begins.

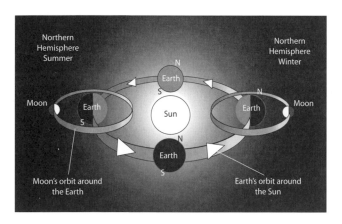

Moon's orbit around the Earth

Northern Hemisphere Summer

Northern Hemisphere Winter

Earth's orbit around the Sun

C ¹²Many of the planets in the solar system have smaller satellites, or **moons**, that orbit them. ¹³Earth has only one moon, which is made of rock and dust. ¹⁴It is about one-quarter of the size of Earth. ¹⁵The moon revolves around Earth once every 28 days (approximately one month) at a distance of 238,866 miles (384,400 km). ¹⁶The moon is kept in orbit by Earth's gravitational pull. ¹⁷It appears to be different shapes as it moves around Earth because the size of the lighted part we see from Earth changes. ¹⁸The **phases** you see depend on the positions of the moon, Earth, and the sun. ¹⁹Only one side of the moon is

visible from Earth because it rotates in the same length of time that it takes to revolve around Earth. ²⁰This is called captured motion.

D ²¹The sun and moon pull on Earth, its ocean waters, and even you! ²²Since the moon is almost 400 times closer to Earth, it exerts more pull on the oceans than the sun. ²³The moon's pull is stronger on the water closer to it, which creates a swell, or **high tide**. ²⁴On the opposite side of Earth, the moon's pull is weaker and forms another high tide. ²⁵The **low** tides are found midway between the high tides. ²⁶Study the diagram below of Earth's tides. ²⁷You can see that Earth becomes somewhat egg-shaped from the force of gravity, which causes high tides on the "front and back" of Earth (as seen from the moon) and low tides on the sides.

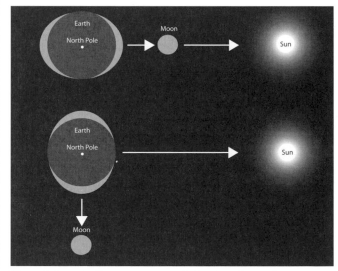

²⁸Earth's rotations are much faster than the moon's orbit, which is what causes the low and high tides to occur twice per day.

E ²⁹Eclipses occur when Earth and the moon pass through each other's shadows. ³⁰Lunar eclipses happen when the moon passes through Earth's shadow and doesn't get sunlight for a short period of time. ³¹Solar eclipses happen when Earth is in the moon's shadow and the sunlight is blocked from Earth for a short time.

1. For each statement, circle T for true and F for false. If the statement is false, replace the **bold word(s)** to make the statement true. Then write the number of the sentence(s) that best supports the answer.

   a. T   F   It takes Earth **24 hours** to revolve around the sun. _____

   _____

   b. T   F   The moon revolves around Earth once every **year**. _____

   _____

   c. T   F   It takes **one day** for Earth to rotate once on its axis. _____

   _____

   d. T   F   **Lunar eclipses** occur when the full moon passes through Earth's shadow. _____

   _____

2. The International Date Line is:
   a. where daylight changes to night.
   b. the line of longitude on the globe that is considered the location where a new day begins.
   c. a place where one season changes to another.
   d. a place on the globe where east changes to west.

   Write the number of the sentence that best supports the answer. _____

3. The path in which Earth moves around the sun is a(n):
   a. rotation.
   b. axis.
   c. ellipse.
   d. cycle.

   Write the number of the sentence that best supports the answer. _____

4. Refer to the lesson and diagram to explain why the moon keeps the same face toward Earth.

   _____

   _____

   _____

Write the numbers of the sentences that best support the answer. _____, _____

5. How does a solar eclipse compare to a lunar eclipse?

   _____

   _____

   _____

   _____

Write the numbers of the sentences that best support the answer. _____, _____

6. Complete the Venn diagram to compare Earth and the moon.

   Earth   Moon

   The moon shines because it is reflecting the sun's light. What we see from Earth depends on the angle at which the sun's light is hitting the moon.

7. Refer to the box above and on the next page to explain why a person on Earth cannot see the moon during the new moon phase.

   _____

   _____

   _____

   _____

8. Using the same diagram, explain why the moon seems to change shape during a month.

   _____

   _____

   _____

   _____

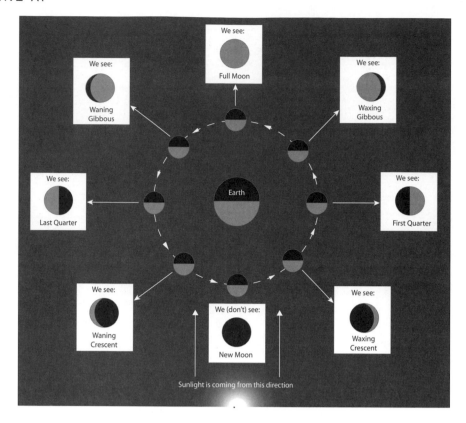

Written Response Questions

For the following two questions, apply all of the information you have learned when answering.

9. How does Earth's rotation cause day and night?

_____

_____

_____

_____

_____

_____

10. Imagine that Earth was not tilted on its axis. What might happen to the seasons?

_____

_____

_____

_____

_____

_____

43. Weather: Measurement, Causes, and Changes

A [1]**Weather** affects our lives every day. [2]Weather appears as sunshine, cloud cover, temperature, wind, rain, drought, frost, snow, and ice. [3]It usually determines what we will wear for the day and maybe what activities we do. [4]It also affects agriculture, sports, transportation, and industry.

B [5]Weather is the condition of the atmosphere near Earth's surface. [6]Weather changes because of the constant changes in the atmosphere. [7]The **troposphere**, the lowest layer of the atmosphere, is where most water is found and where most clouds form.

C [8]The sun plays the most important role in causing weather. [9]Heat from the sun warms up Earth and, in turn, the heat from Earth's warmed surface passes back into the air. [10]The sun's rays have the strongest effect on the middle of Earth (the equator) where the rays hit it directly and the **ozone layer** of the atmosphere is thinner. [11]This warm air then rises and cool air flows in to take its place. [12]This air movement is what causes **wind** in the atmosphere. [13]The heating and movement of air over the equator forces air to move in northern and southern directions, forming the global wind patterns. [14]These winds are called the **trade winds**.

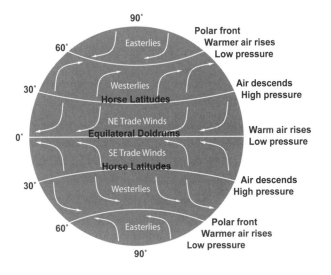

D [15]Meteorologists use **barometers** to measure **air pressure**, which is created by the atmosphere pressing down on Earth's surface. [16]The amount of pressure air exerts is influenced by the temperature, amount of water vapor, volume, and height of the air above Earth. [17]Air pressure is constantly changing and helps to predict what kind of weather to expect. [18]If a **high-pressure system** is forecast, then cooler weather and clear skies are coming. [19]A prediction of a **low-pressure system** will bring warm weather, storms, and rain.

E [20]Relative **humidity** is the amount of moisture in the air and is also important in the description of weather conditions. [21]The amount of humidity in the air is measured using a **psychrometer**. [22]Water exists in Earth's atmosphere as water vapor that comes from oceans, rivers, lakes, plants, and many other places. [23]The sun heats the water on Earth and changes it into a gas called **water vapor** through **evaporation**. [24]When the air is cooled high up in the atmosphere, the water vapor turns into liquid droplets of water or ice and forms clouds. [25]This process is called **condensation**. [26]When the cloud droplets or ice crystals become heavy enough, gravity pulls this moisture to Earth as **precipitation** in the form of rain, hail, sleet, or snow. [27]This whole process is known as the **water cycle**.

F [28]Weather conditions also change throughout the year because of Earth's tilt on its axis and its orbit around the sun. [29]This is what causes the seasons.

G [30]Weather may change from day to day and season to season. [31]Year after year, weather conditions are usually repeated in the same area. [32]This repeating pattern of weather in a particular area is what makes up that area's climate. [33]**Climate** is the weather that characterizes a particular region over a period of time.

1. For each statement, circle T for true and F for false. If the statement is false, replace the **bold word(s)** to make the statement true. Then write the number of the sentence(s) that best supports the answer.

   a. T F Most of Earth's weather occurs in the **troposphere**. _____

   _____

   b. T F If a **high-pressure system** is forecast, then warm weather, storms, and rain can be expected. _____

   _____

   c. T F Rain or snow is called **condensation**. _____

   _____

   d. T F **Psychrometers** measure air pressure. _____

   _____

2. Wind is caused by air:
   a. moving because warm air is rising and cool air is flowing in to take its place.
   b. moving from land to sea.
   c. moving from an area of low pressure to an area of high pressure.
   d. moving from sea to land.

   Write the number of the sentence that best supports the answer. _____

3. The troposphere differs from other layers of the atmosphere because of its concentration of which gas?
   a. nitrogen
   b. oxygen
   c. carbon dioxide
   d. water vapor

   Write the number of the sentence that best supports the answer. _____

4. Weather affects our lives every day. What is the difference between weather and climate?

   _____

   _____

   _____

Write the numbers of the sentences that best support the answer. _____, _____

5. How do meteorologists use changing air pressure to predict weather?

   _____

   _____

   _____

   _____

Write the numbers of the sentences that best support the answer.
_____, _____

6. How does the location of a place near the equator affect its weather?

   _____

   _____

   _____

   _____

Write the number of the sentence that best supports the answer.

_____

7. Explain the relationship between the water cycle and weather.

   _____

   _____

   _____

   _____

   _____

BEAUFORT WIND SCALE

#	m/s		Common signs for recognition
0	0-1		Smoke rises vertically
1	1-2		Smoke drifts slowly
2	2-3		Leaves just move
3	4-5		Leaves move constantly
4	6-8		Small branches move
5	9-11		Small trees sway
6	12-14		Large branches sway
7	15-17		Large trees sway
8	18-20		Small branches break
9	21-24		Large branches break
10	25-28		Small trees uprooted

The Beaufort Scale was designed to estimate wind speed when an anemometer (an instrument used to measure wind speed) is not available.

8. Do you think the Beaufort Scale could have any use in the world today? Explain.

_____

_____

_____

_____

_____

Written Response Questions

For the following two questions, apply all of the information you have learned when answering.

9. Name two instruments meteorologists use to observe and measure weather conditions and explain how they are used.

_____

_____

_____

_____

_____

_____

10. What is the relationship between the sun and wind?

_____

_____

_____

_____

44. Classification of the Sun and Other Stars

A [1]The numerous stars shining in the night sky are just a fraction of the stars in the universe. [2]There are billions of them, including our sun.

B [3]The sun is Earth's closest **star** and is located at the center of the solar system. [4]All of the planets revolve around it because of its huge gravitational force. [5]Although the sun appears larger than anything else in the solar system, it is considered only a medium-sized star.

C [6]The sun is made of hot gases called plasma. [7]Many people believe the sun is a hot ball of burning gases, but it's not. [8]The plasma that makes up the sun is actually so hot that it glows much like a wire in a light bulb. [9]About three-quarters of the sun is made of hydrogen and one-quarter is helium. [10]It produces energy through **nuclear fusion** reactions (a process by which the nuclei of two or more atoms join to form a single, larger nucleus) that turn hydrogen atoms into helium atoms. [11]This energy radiates through space and provides Earth with the heat and light necessary to maintain life. [12]The sun's light is so powerful that it can damage your eyesight even from Earth.

D [13]Solar energy is created deep within the **core** of the sun, where the temperature is 27,000,000 degrees Fahrenheit (15,000,000 degrees Celsius). [14]Heat from the core travels through the **radiation** and **convection zones** to the surface of the sun. [15]It takes a million years for the energy generated in the sun's core to reach its surface.

E [16]The next layer of the sun that gives off the light energy that is seen from Earth is called the **photosphere**. [17]It is the innermost layer of the sun's atmosphere and glows at more than 9,900 degrees Fahrenheit (5,500 degrees Celsius). [18]That's hot enough to melt almost any substance. [19]**Sunspots**, which are small, dark patches that are cooler than the surrounding areas, are located in this layer of the sun.

F [20]The atmospheric layer above the photosphere is the **chromosphere**. [21]The **corona** is the outermost layer of the sun's atmosphere. [22]**Solar prominences**, huge blazes of gas, appear in this area along with **solar flares**, which are fierce, brilliant explosions of gas.

G [23]Stars are categorized by their **brightness**, **color**, and **temperature**. [24]These characteristics may change through a star's life cycle. [25]Scientists use a scale called **magnitude** to measure their brightness. [26]The brightest stars give off the most energy. [27]The star's size, temperature, and distance from Earth are important factors for how bright a star looks, known as its **apparent magnitude**. [28]The sun appears to be the brightest star from Earth, but using the magnitude scale, scientists are able to make a more accurate measurement of its brightness. [29]The brightest stars are classified as 0 (or even minus magnitudes) and the dimmest stars can have a magnitude as high as 9.

H [30]The color of a star depends on its surface temperature. [31]Stars are classified according to their colors or **spectral type**. [32]Red stars are the coolest, orange and yellow stars are somewhat hotter, and the hottest stars are blue or blue-white.

I [33]Early astronomers studied patterns of bright stars called constellations. [34]Many of the constellations are named after characters or objects from ancient Greek myths. [35]As Earth spins, the constellations appear to move, too.

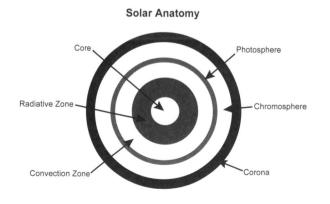

Solar Anatomy

Core

Photosphere

Radiative Zone

Chromosphere

Convection Zone

Corona

1. For each statement, circle T for true and F for false. If the statement is false, replace the **bold word(s)** to make the statement true. Then write the number of the sentence(s) that best supports the answer.
   a. T F The sun is considered to be a **large** star in the solar system. ____

   _____

   b. T F The sun is a hot ball of **burning gases**. ____

   _____

   c. T F It takes **a million years** for the energy generated in the sun's core to reach its surface. ____

   _____

   d. T F Scientists use a scale called magnitude to measure a star's **heat**. ____

   _____

2. What do astronomers call the patterns that we see in the sky?
   a. galaxies
   b. solar systems
   c. constellations
   d. moons

   Write the number of the sentence that best supports the answer. ____

3. The brightness of a star is its:
   a. spectral type.
   b. magnitude.
   c. corona.
   d. flare.

   Write the number of the sentence that best supports the answer. ____

4. What is the relationship between a star's temperature and its brightness?

   _____

   _____

   _____

   _____

Write the numbers of the sentences that best support the answer. ____, ____

5. What are three ways stars are categorized?

   _____

   _____

   _____

Write the number of the sentence that best supports the answer. ____

6. Describe nuclear fusion reactions as they occur in the sun.

   _____

   _____

   _____

   _____

   _____

Write the numbers of the sentences that best support the answer. ____, ____

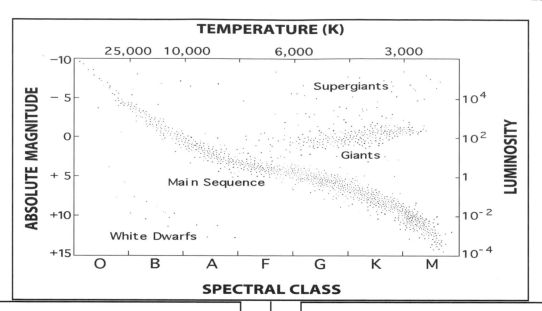

In the early 1900s, two astronomers, Ejnar Hertzsprung and Henry Russell, tried to find a pattern in the life of stars. They tried to see if there was a relationship between a star's brightness and its temperature. This chart is called the Hertzsprung-Russell (H-R) diagram. An H-R diagram compares the temperatures and absolute magnitudes of stars.

The diagram shows the largest stars at the top and the smallest stars at the bottom. The bluest (hotter) stars are on the left, and the reddest (cooler) stars are on the right. The stars that are near the top of the chart are the brightest and those near the bottom are the dimmest.

8. According to the diagram, what is the range of absolute magnitude for a supergiant?

_____

_____

7. If you were looking at the night sky, what type of star would you most likely see?

_____

_____

Written Response Questions

For the following two questions, apply all of the information you have learned when answering.

9. What are the layers of the sun and what are they made of?

_____

_____

_____

_____

10. Why does the sun have spots?

_____

_____

_____

_____

45. Inner and Outer Solar System

A [1]The **solar system** is made up of the sun, the eight official planets, at least three dwarf planets, more than 130 satellites of the planets, comets, asteroids, dust, cosmic rays, and hot plasma.

B [2]The **inner solar system** contains Mercury, Venus, Earth, and Mars because they are the planets closest to the sun. [3]They are known as **terrestrial planets** because of their solid, rocky surfaces.

C [4]As you can see from the diagram, **Mercury** is very small and is the closest planet to the sun. [5]This makes its orbits around the sun shorter than the orbit of any other planet. [6]Unlike the other planets, Mercury has a minimal atmosphere, which is made up of just traces of hydrogen and helium. [7]Its temperature can reach 800 degrees Fahrenheit (400 degrees Celsius). [8]That's more than four times hotter than boiling water!

D [9]**Venus**, the second planet from the sun, is similar in size to Earth. [10]Its surface is mainly flat with some craters and active volcanoes. [11]The atmosphere is made up largely of carbon dioxide gas that presses down on the surface with great weight. [12]Its dense clouds are made up of sulfuric acids that reflect the sun's rays. [13]Next to the sun and moon, Venus is the brightest object in the sky and is hotter than Mercury, even though it's farther from the sun.

E [14]The third planet from the sun is **Earth** and the fourth is **Mars**. [15]Mars is sometimes called the Red Planet because it's covered with reddish-orange dust. [16]It has many rocky canyons and craters and is only half the size of Earth.

F [17]The **outer solar system** contains Jupiter, Saturn, Uranus, and Neptune. [18]They are sometimes called the **Jovian** (Jupiterlike) **Planets** or the **gas giants** because they are mostly made of gas, although some, or maybe all of them, may have small, solid cores.

G [19]**Jupiter**, the largest planet, is almost 1,500 times the size of Earth and is twice as heavy as all of the other planets put together. [20]It is mostly made of hydrogen and helium gas, but because of its great mass, its gravity squeezes the gases together so that they act like a liquid near the center, where it has a solid, rocky core. [21]The **Great Red Spot**, located on the surface, is really an enormous storm.

H [22]The second-largest planet in the solar system is **Saturn**. [23]It is made mostly of liquid and solid hydrogen and helium, which makes it very light compared to the other planets. [24]It is usually called the **Ringed Planet** because of the rings of dust, ice, and rocks that surround it. [25]By using space probes, scientists now know that many other planets have rings, also.

I [26]**Uranus** is four times as wide as Earth and 14 times bigger. [27]Unlike the other planets that spin upright around the sun, Uranus rolls on its side. [28]The days and nights each last for 42 years on this planet. [29]Uranus also has rings around it that are made up of dark dust.

J [30]**Neptune**, the smallest planet, appears pale blue because it is made of methane, helium, and ammonia gases. [31]It may also have an outer layer of liquid hydrogen. [32]Neptune is the farthest planet from the sun.

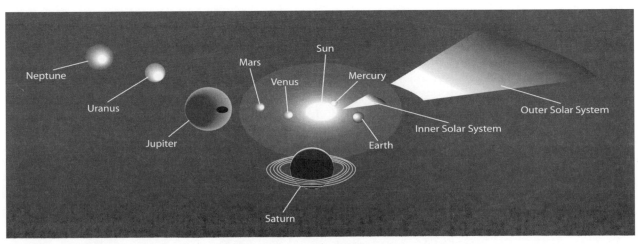

1. For each statement, circle T for true and F for false. If the statement is false, replace the **bold word(s)** to make the statement true. Then write the number of the sentence(s) that best supports the answer.
   a. T F The **outer solar system** contains the terrestrial planets. _____ , _____

   _____

   b. T F **Venus** is the brightest object in the sky and is hotter than Mercury. _____

   _____

   c. T F **Mars** is sometimes called the Red Planet because it's covered with reddish-orange dust. _____

   _____

   d. T F **Neptune** is the farthest planet from the sun. _____

   _____

2. Which planet is similar in size to Earth?
   a. Mars
   b. Jupiter
   c. Venus
   d. Saturn

   Write the number of the sentence that best supports the answer. _____

3. What are the rings around Saturn made up of?
   a. dust
   b. rocks
   c. ice
   d. all of the above

   Write the number of the sentence that best supports the answer. _____

4. What makes up our solar system?

   _____

   _____

   _____

   Write the number of the sentence that best supports the answer. _____

5. How are the outer planets alike?

   _____

   _____

   _____

   _____

   Write the numbers of the sentences that best support the answer. _____ , _____

6. What is the Great Red Spot and where is it?

   _____

   _____

   _____

   _____

   Write the number of the sentence that best supports the answer. _____

The following table lists statistical information about the planets:

Planet	Distance From the Sun (in millions of km)	Distance Across (in km)	Length of Year (in Earth days)
Earth	150	12,750	365
Jupiter	778	143,000	4,380
Mars	228	6,800	730
Mercury	58	4,900	88
Neptune	4,505	49,000	60,225
Saturn	1,427	120,000	10,585
Uranus	2,869	51,000	30,660
Venus	108	12,000	225

7. Complete the chart using information from the lesson and diagrams.

Closest to Sun to Farthest From Sun	Smallest to Largest	Shortest Year to Longest Year

8. Using the chart you just completed, what can you infer about this data?

_____

_____

_____

_____

_____

Written Response Questions

For the following two questions, apply all of the information you have learned when answering.

9. How are the inner planets different from the outer planets?

_____

_____

_____

_____

_____

_____

10. What is unique about Earth compared to the other inner planets?

_____

_____

_____

_____

_____

_____

_____

ANSWERS

1. Measuring Matter: Mass, Volume, and Density, p. 2

1. a. T (1,3)

   b. F (7), weight

   c. F (36), stays the same

   d. F (18), 30 cm³

2. d

3. b

4. 10x4x3=120 cm³

5. 2 g/cm³ (32)

6. Answers will vary, but they need to equal 60 when the numbers are multiplied, such as 15 x 2 x 2 = 60 or 5 x 6 x 2 = 60.

7.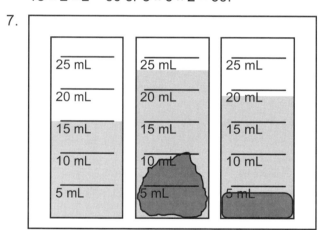

8. a. 7 g/cm³

   b. 9 g/cm³

9. Martha should measure the tub's length, width, and height. Then she should multiply these dimensions to find the tub's volume. Example: If the tub measures 6 ft by 3 ft by 2.5 ft, then the tub's volume is 45 ft³.

10. Don should use some type of measuring cup, such as a graduated cylinder. He should fill the cylinder with water to a starting amount, such as 20 mL. Then, after he places the keys in the water, he should see how much the water rose. This displaced amount is the volume of the keys. Example: If the water rises to 24 mL, then the volume of the keys is 4 mL.

2. Physical and Chemical Properties of Matter, p. 5

1. a. F (2), unique or different

   b. T (12, 13, 15)

   c. T (39)

   d. T (19)

2. d (9)

3. b

4. Properties should be listed that use the senses and other properties listed in this lesson, such as:
   a. Rose- fragrant, thorny stem, soft
   b. Basketball- sphere, bouncy, rubbery, buoyant in water
   c. Metal cooking pan- luster, conductivity, smooth
   d. Ice cube- solid form of water, cold, transparent, freezing/melting point of zero degrees C

5. Gasoline and ethyl alcohol are less dense than pure water, so they are buoyant. (12, 13)

6. The other substances have a greater density than pure water, so they are not buoyant in pure water.

7. They are ductile, malleable, and have luster.

8. It tarnishes.

9. The water would evaporate. The powdery orange drink would crystallize and remain in the glass.

10. Since saltwater has a lower freezing point than pure water, the salt lowers the freezing point of the snow and ice, causing it to melt.

3. Physical and Chemical Changes in Matter, p. 8

1. a. F (21, 22), condensation

   b. T (17)

   c. F (25), can be reversed

   d. F (11, 12), different melting points

2. c

3. c (39, 41)

4. The unmixed suspension should show all parts separated in layers. The mixed suspension should show all parts in different areas of the container, not in layers.

5. Condensation is gas changing to a liquid and evaporation is liquid changing to gas. (15, 21)

6. Answers will vary. The chart below shows possible answers:

Changes		
Objects	**Physical**	**Chemical**
apple	cut into pieces	pieces turn brown
leaf	animal bite	changing color
egg and milk	blend together	cook into scrambled eggs
cheese	softens	grows mold
paper bag	rips	catches on fire

7. Solution Chart:

Solution	Solute	Solvent
Saltwater	salt	water
Orange Drink	orange powder	water
Chocolate Milk	chocolate powder	milk

8. The candlewick burning is a chemical change because the burning is changing the chemicals in the wick. I can tell because the wick changes color, I see light energy, I feel heat energy, and I can even smell the burning odor. The wax melting is a physical change because melting is a physical change; the liquid wax can cool and harden again into the same solid wax substance.

9. Most steps of preparation will be physical changes. The main chemical changes should be the pancake mixture cooking, rising, and even burning.

4. Atoms, Elements, and Compounds, p. 11

1. a. T (4)

   b. F (7), the same chemical properties

   c. F (18), different properties

   d. F (35), 13

2. d

3. d (8)

4. The positive particles in the center of the atom should be labeled as protons. The other particles in the center of the atom should be labeled as neutrons. The negative particles circling the nucleus should be labeled as electrons. (8, 9, 10)

5. Atoms carry no net charge because the **neutrons** carry a neutral charge and there are equal quantities of positively charged **protons** and negatively charged **electrons**.

6.
11
Na
23

7. a. 8

   b. 12

   c. 10

   d. 10

   e. 7

8. The fluorine atom diagram should have a nucleus with 9 protons and 9 or more neutrons with 9 electrons circling the nucleus.

9. The carbon atom diagram should have a nucleus with 6 protons and 6 or more neutrons with 6 electrons circling the nucleus.

10. The salt may be described as solid, hard crystals. More may be described about the look or even taste of the salt. The differences between sodium and chlorine and salt include the color (both), state of matter (chlorine is a gas) and being non-edible due to being poisonous (chlorine).

5. Chemicals: Helpful and Harmful, p. 14

1. a. F (19), dangerous to taste, smell, and touch

   b. T (2)

   c. F (24), the closer to 1 or 14

   d. T (20)

2. d (13, 15)

3. c

4. The presence of acid decreases.

5. <u>Avoid</u>: lemons, oranges, grapefruits, soft drinks, foods with vinegar, tomatoes, grapes, coffee <u>Eat</u>: eggs, milk, water

6. It would taste bitter. (17, 18)

7. a. light red (12)

    b. Human blood has a pH level of about 9, which means it is a base. Human saliva has a pH level of about 7, which is neutral.

8. The containers should be labeled with four of the following chemicals: sodium hydroxide, lye, oven cleaner, bleach, ammonia, soap, hydrochloric acid, battery acid, or lemon juice.

9. Some points that should be made about these chemicals: They are deadly, toxic, dangerous if tasted, smelled, or touched; extreme acids and extreme bases are hazardous; keep them out of reach of children.

10. Two of the following should be explained: Oven cleaner is used for cleaning ovens, bleach is used for whitening fabric, chlorine (in small amounts) is used for keeping pool water clean and killing germs in drinking water, baking soda is used in baking food, and battery acid is used to keep batteries working.

6. Kinetic and Potential Energy, p. 17

1. a. T (4)

    b. T (10,11)

    c. F (18, 21), is not demonstrating work

    d. F (9), will not always

2. b

3. c

4. a. At the highest point of the swing (13, 15)

    b. No, there is not any kinetic energy because it is not in motion at this point. The energy was changed to gravitational potential energy. (4, 13)

5. 25 × 10 = 250 joules

6. 50 × 12 = 600 joules

7. The acorns on the highest branch would have more potential energy because energy is gained by the height of the object above the ground.

8. The energy becomes kinetic energy because the rubber band is moving.

9. The example needs to involve someone moving an object over a distance. The formula W=FXD should be used to calculate the amount of work done.

10. The example needs to involve someone applying force but not moving an object.

7. Force and Motion, p. 20

1. a. T (4)

    b. F (12), inertia

    c. T (21)

    d. F (21), decrease

2. c (32, 33)

3. c (23, 24, 26)

4. kinetic friction (or sliding friction) (8)

5. a. Examples of forces will vary. Possible examples: friction, a hand, the ground

    b. Newton's first law of motion (law of inertia)

6. The moving car exerts a force on the tree in one direction and the tree exerts a force on the car in the other. The car hit the tree with force and the tree pushed back on the car with equal force.

7. No. If the smaller bike has a greater speed, it could have more momentum than the larger bike. (28, 30)

8.

Newton's Laws of Motion	
Newton's <u>third</u> law of motion	This law explains action and <u>reaction.</u>
Newton's <u>second</u> law of motion	This law explains that force causes objects to <u>accelerate.</u>
Newton's <u>first</u> law of motion	This is the law of <u>inertia.</u>

9. Answers will vary. The name of the law and an explanation should be given.

10. One suggestion could be to remove some of the mass in the wagon by having a child get out. The other suggestion could be to increase the force by asking someone to help push or pull the wagon.

8. Simple Machines: Inclined Plane, Lever, Machines, and Work, p. 23

1. a. T (6)
   b. T (27)
   c. F (31), all levers do not have
   d. F (11), don't do less work (or) do the same amount of work

2. a

3. d

4. a. 4 × 500=2,000 joules of work
   b. 10 × 200=2,000 joules of work
   c. They both did the same amount of work.
   d. Less effort is used when pushing the load up the ramp. (10)

5. Answers will vary. The wedge should be named, drawn, and marked as single or double wedge.

6. 1st class levers (28, 32)

7. The diagram of a seesaw should show the stiff bar of the lever with the fulcrum in the middle. The effort and load can be on either end or both ends.

8. Screw or inclined plane. The spiral of the bottle-head is a modified inclined plane that wraps around to screw the cap in place.

9. Answers will vary. An explanation of how this inclined plane is useful should be given.

10. Answers will vary. The load, effort, and fulcrum should be included in the explanation of how this lever is used. The lever's class should be named.

9. Simple Machines: Wheel-and-Axle and Pulley, p. 26

1. a. F (18), sometimes pull in the same direction
   b. T (13)
   c. T (2)

d. F (21), a combination of fixed and movable pulleys

2. d (9)

3. c

4. With a movable pulley, only half the effort force is used. (19)

5. With a fixed pulley, you are pulling down and working with gravity. (13)

6. The wheel, axle, and fulcrum should be labeled on both the Ferris wheel and a drawn diagram of a doorknob.

7. The distance that we pull the load is increased. (26)

8. A: 4

   B: 3

   C: 8

9. The first pulley is a fixed pulley, which contains only one pulley and is attached to a base. It works by using gravity and by pulling down. The second pulley is a compound pulley, which has a fixed pulley and a movable pulley working as a system. It uses the same amount of force as the movable pulley and has the effort force in the same direction as the fixed pulley.

10. In the first picture, the man is using all of his effort to lift the bag. In the second picture, the man is using a fixed pulley, which requires less effort because he is pulling down instead of lifting up. In the third picture, the man is using a compound pulley, which reduces the effort to half the effort required by the fixed pulley.

10. Thermal Energy, p. 29

1. a. F (32), insulator
   b. F (4), vibrate or push and pull
   c. T (16, 20, 25); d. T (4,9,12)

2. b

3. a

4. temperature = thermal energy < (14, 15)

5. cool (21)

6. radiation; the baking of a cake is a chemical change

7. conduction; the hot oatmeal transferred heat to the solid bowl

8. convection; the lake water must be warmer than the air, causing the air above the water to warm and rise, bringing in cooler air that Travis felt as a breeze. This is called convection current.

9. The answer should include two insulators such as a jacket, gloves, sleeping bag, blankets, thermos, etc., for preventing heat from transferring. The answer should also include two conductors: any metal items, because heat transfers easily through metal.

10. The particles of the solid wax candle are close together, pushing, pulling, and vibrating but not moving away from their place. As the wax melts, the particles are moving faster and flowing around each other because the melted wax is liquid.

11. Sound and Light Energy, p. 32

1. a. T (19, 20)

   b. F (17), at very different speeds

   c. F (13), sound waves

   d. T (28)

2. c

3. c

4. a. transparent

   b. translucent

   c. translucent

   d. opaque

   e. opaque

   f. transparent (20, 24, 25)

5. Slow vibrations have a low frequency and low-pitched sound. (11,12)

6. Light colored items would be easier to see, because the lighter color would reflect light while a darker color would absorb the light. (31)

7.

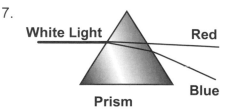

8. Answers will vary, but two facts about sound and/or light energy should be written and explanations should be given for why they are interesting.

9. When the cabinet door was closed, the molecules in the cabinet and the air around it vibrated, which caused sound waves. The vibrations continued to spread through the particles in the air to Monica's ear.

10. The green leaf appears green because it is absorbing all the other colors except green. The green light reflects back to your eye.

12. Static Electricity, p. 35

1. a. T (31)

   b. T (18)

   c. F (17), electrons

   d. F (11), is not always required

2. d (24, 26)

3. c (21)

4. Negative charges in the lower part of the cloud are attracted to the positively charged ground below.

5. The fly away hair is actually positively charged hairs that are pushing away from each other. Therefore, the loose hairs are flying away from each other.

6. The head hugging hair is where static electricity has developed so the electrons are attracted to the protons. Therefore, the hair is clinging to the head.

7. a. Standing in open field: A person standing in an open field is higher than everything around, and the body is a good conductor of electricity.

   b. Golfers on golf course: The same conditions exist as in an open field, and golfers hold metal golf clubs that are also good conductors.

   c. Person driving tractor: The tractor is a large metal piece of equipment, making it a good conductor of electricity.

8. (with 7)

9. When Olivia walked over to Grant, she was probably wearing socks that slid along the carpeting. This caused electrons to rub off of the floor and onto Olivia, making her

negatively charged. When she reached out to touch Grant, the electrons from her hand were attracted to the protons on his shoulder, and this caused the electrons to jump to his shoulder as a spark.   If Grant did not rub his feet on the floor like Olivia did, then he did not build up electrons in his body.

10. The diagram should show a hand reaching to a shoulder and a spark between the hand and the shoulder. The hand should have negative (-) electron symbols. The shoulder should have a mix of positive (+) protons and negative (-) electrons with more of the protons near the edge with the spark. The spark should have negative (-) electron symbols.

13. Circuits, p. 38

1. a. F (9), through the complete circuit back to its starting point

   b. F (14), a resistor

   c. F (16), opening a switch

   d. F (21), a parallel circuit

2. b

3. b (18, 19)

4. a parallel circuit (22)

5. A: 8 amps

   B: 7 ohms

   C: 84 volts

   D: 5 ohms

   E: 135 volts

   F: 13 amps

6. a. circuit F

   b. circuit F

   c. circuit D

   d. circuit A

7. The top symbol should be labeled as the battery, the bottom symbol should be labeled as the resistor, and the symbol to the right should be labeled as the switch. The straight lines could also be labeled as the wires or conductors.

8. The series circuit should have one path with one battery symbol and three resistor symbols.

9. The parallel circuit should have two or more paths with one battery symbol, four resistor symbols, and two switch symbols.

10. Answers will vary, but the student should name three resistor items such as light, TV, computer, etc. There should also be an explanation of the type of energy that these resistors transform to.

14. Electromagnets, p. 41

1. a. T (29)

   b. F (15), very easy devices

   c. F (14), a device that becomes magnetic when an electric current flows through coiled wire in a circuit

   d. T (6)

2. d

3. d

4. Electromagnets can easily change strength and be turned on and off. (23, 24)

5. Gather a battery, wire, and nail or other metal bar. Wrap the wire several times around the nail. Connect the two wires to the + and – ends of the battery. (15, 16)

6. Two additional magnets should be drawn up against the magnet given with opposite poles touching: N to S and S to N (5, 6)

7. approx. 100 and approx. 190

8. The higher the voltage of the battery, the higher the strength of the electromagnet will be. The more coils, the higher the strength of the electromagnet will be.

9. Answers will vary. Explanation should be made that the napkin is not made of metal, and, therefore, it would not be attracted to a magnet. Recommendations should be made to increase the number of coils and/or the voltage of the battery on the electromagnet in order to pick up the large paperclip.

10. Moving electric charges create a magnetic field, which is called electromagnetism. Electrical appliances have magnets within their motors.

15. Electric Energy, p. 44

1. a. T (5, 6)

   b. F (14), some turbines

   c. T (8)

   d. F (22), decrease voltage

2. a

3. d

4. because it reverses direction (16)

5. a. 60 × 10 = 600 cycles

   b. 60 × 60 = 3,600 cycles (17)

6. 10,000 - 1,200 = 8,800 V

7. 732,174 – 732,068 = 106 kilowatt-hours

8. Answers will vary. Answers should explain ways to save on electricity at home, such as turning off the lights, TV, computer, etc.

9. The turbine is a wheel that spins the shaft that turns the coil on a generator. Using alternating current, the generator produces electricity.

10. The transformer decreases the electric current coming from the high power lines to the commercial power lines. Then another transformer decreases the amount of electric current even more as it travels to residential power lines.

16. Energy Sources and Conversion, p. 47

1. a. T (21, 22)

   b. F (3), convert several times

   c. T (17)

   d. F (23), never gone (or lost) completely, only changed (or converted).

2. a

3. d

4. Food is converted into chemical energy in your body. The chemical energy is converted into mechanical energy and heat energy. (7, 8, 9)

5. It takes a very long time for fossil fuels to form under Earth's surface, so they are considered nonrenewable resources. Once they are gone, we cannot get them back. (13, 14)

6. The solar energy from the sun heats the solar collectors on the solar panel. The cool water is pumped to the heat exchanger and then through the solar panel area. This warms the water, which is then pumped back through the heat exchanger and then back to the pool.

7. Answers will vary but may include: don't need to worry about batteries running out of power; can be stored in an emergency box for a long time.

8. Mechanical Energy – Electromagnetic Energy – Light Energy

9. Answers will vary, but the answer should include energy conversion, beginning with solar energy.

10. Energy from the sun is converted to light energy, which is converted to chemical energy in the plant. The plant is consumed by a person who converts the plant energy to chemical energy in his or her body, which is converted to mechanical energy in order to move the box.

17. Cells, p. 52

1. a. T (1)

   b. T (10)

   c. T (24)

   d. T (35)

2. c (25)

3. d

4. Anton van Leeuwenhoek was the first to observe living single-celled bacteria and paramecia. By the 1800s, better microscopes helped scientists combine their studies of cells into a theory. Schleiden and Schwann stated that all living things are made of cells. Rudolf Virchow also contributed to The Cell Theory because he concluded that cells don't form on their own.

5. Prokaryotes were on Earth first and, for billions of years, were the only form of life. They are single-celled organisms with no defined nucleus that can live on their own. Eukaryotes are more advanced than prokaryotes because each of their cells has a true nucleus inside a membrane. (23, 24, 27)

6. Answers will vary.

7. Cells were not observed before the 1600s because microscopes weren't invented until 1665.

8. Blood cells are different from skin cells because they have different functions to perform.

9.-10. 1665-Robert Hooke invented the microscope.

 1673-Anton van Leeuwenhoek observed living single-celled bacteria and paramecia.

 1800s-Matthias Schleiden and Theodor Schwann stated that all living things are made of cells.

 1815 (approx.)-Rudolf Virchow concluded that cells don't form on their own.

18. Cell Parts and Functions, p. 55

1. a. T (7)

 b. T (13)

 c. F (28), plant

 d. T (29)

2. b (9)

3. d (2)

4. Only plant cells contain a cell wall and chloroplasts. (28)

5. The nucleus contains DNA and controls all cell activities. (9)

6. The three main parts are the cell membrane, the nucleus, and the cytoplasm. (6, 7, 10)

7. The cell membrane is an outer covering that gives the cell shape and helps control materials that move in and out of the cell.

8. perfume, tea bag in water, food coloring

9. Plant cell: cell wall chloroplasts;
 Both: nucleus, cell membrane, cytoplasm, mitochondria, vacuoles, ribosomes, lysosomes

10. Cell parts perform specific functions to operate like a factory. Each part of the cell has a special job to make the cell work properly.

19. Reproduction and Growth of Cells, p. 58

1. a. T (4)

 b. F (28), meiosis

 c. F (13), asexual

 d. T (30)

2. c (13)

3. b (29)

4. meiosis: one sex cell divides into four instead of two, and each new cell has half of the number of chromosomes
 mitosis: the nucleus of the cell divides and then the cell divides into two identical cells

5.-6. Diagrams will vary.

7. Answers will vary.

8. Humans are born, they grow and develop, and they die. Cells form new cells, which grow and develop. Some become worn out and die while others divide to form more new cells.

9. The female parent egg cell and the male parent sperm cell joined together to form a new cell called a zygote, which is the first cell of a new organism. It has one complete set of chromosomes. The zygote will continue to divide by mitosis to form the many cells that will make up the adult body of the organism.

10. Mitosis helps heal a wound when the body cells divide to form two identical cells with an exact copy of the parent cell's chromosomes. Skin cells are constantly dying and being replaced.

20. Genetics, p. 61

1. a. T (1)

 b. F (19), purebred

 c. F (22), geneticists

 d. T (20)

2. b

3. c

4.

	B	b
b	Bb	bb
b	Bb	bb

5. a. 4

   b. black or brown

   c. 50%

   d. 50%

6. AA(Ho)   Bb(He)

   Cc(He)   DD(Ho)

   Ee(He)   ff(Ho)

7. BB: brown eyes

   Bb: brown eyes

   bb: blue eyes

8. Straight hair: SS and Ss

   Curly hair: ss

9. Mendel discovered that crossing two tall pea plants did not always produce tall plants. The plants produced mostly tall plants and some short plants. (E)

10. Each parent has genotype Ee.

	E	e
E	EE	Ee
e	Ee	ee

21. DNA, p. 64

1. a. T (1)

   b. T (1)

   c. F (7), 46

   d. F (23), identical

2. b

3. d (11)

4. DNA is like a twisted ladder or staircase and is made up of the base compounds A and T or G and C. (10, 11, 12)

5. DNA duplicates itself by splitting down the middle to separate the bases. Bases floating in the cell then pair with the appropriate bases to form two new DNA strands. The two new DNA molecules are the same as the original one.

6. Chromosomes act like blueprints for transferring information. (4)

7. Body cells comprise most of the cells in any organism. Sex cells are produced inside the sex organs of adult organisms.

8. Answers may vary but should mention that the incorrect copying might lead to mutations.

9. One fertilized egg splits into two, so each egg has the same DNA.

10. Answers may vary but should include the concept of DNA replication.

22. Uses of Genetics, p. 67

1. a. F (16), gene splicing

   b. T (31)

   c. T (21)

   d. F (28), selective breeding

2. c

3. a

4. Genetic engineering improves medicine, plants, and animals. (2)

5. better crops and healthier, hardier farm animals

6. Gene splicing is cutting the DNA of a gene from one organism and attaching it, or "splicing" it, to the genes of another organism. It may find cures and vaccines for diseases and improve the nutritional value of fruits and vegetables. (15, 16, 21)

7.-8. Answers will vary.

9. Answers will vary.

10. Yes; through gene splicing, scientists are able to develop fruits and vegetables that are more nutritious.

23. Skeletal and Muscular Systems, p. 70

1. a. T (19)

   b. T (12)

   c. F (27), voluntary muscles

   d. F (28), involuntary muscles

2. d (19)

3. b

4. Ball-and-socket joints: allow circular motion like a joystick; hinge joints: allow back-and-forth movement like a door; fixed joints: no movement.

5. Striated muscles are responsible for the movement of your arms and legs. An electrical impulse sent from the brain stimulates the muscle, causing it to contract. This shortens the muscle length, pulls the attached tendon, and causes the bone to move.

6. One muscle contracts to bend a joint and another contracts to straighten it.

7. Compact bone: made up of dense, circular layers of bone, called lamellae, that form the outer layer of all bones; spongy bone: made up of strong, light tissue, which is found in short, flat bones and in the ends of long bones.

8. Answers will vary.

9. Long bones are light and strong and give our body the strength to support its own weight. The bones of the arms and legs are long bones. Short bones, such as those in the wrists and ankles, are small and allow the body to make flexible, defined movements and to maintain good balance. Flat bones are made of two compact layers of bone that are separated by a spongy layer. They are designed to protect the brain and the organs in the chest. Many bones that make up the face, as well as the kneecaps and vertebrae, are irregular bones.

10. Connective tissues hold everything together. There are three types: ligaments, tendons, and cartilage. Ligaments connect bone to bone, while tendons fasten muscle to bone. The rubbery tissue called cartilage is used to bring bones together, to cushion bones, and to coat and protect the tips of bones at joints.

24. Circulatory and Respiratory Systems, p. 73

1. a. F (5), trachea
   b. F (27), bone marrow
   c. T (8)
   d. T (7)

2. b
3. c
4. red blood cells: made in the bone marrow and contain hemoglobin, help to carry oxygen to the body
   white blood cells: disease-fighting and attack intruders that invade the body (27, 29)

5. The heart is divided into four chambers: the right atrium, the right ventricle, the left atrium, and the left ventricle. The right atrium receives oxygen-poor blood from vessels called veins, and this blood is pumped into the right ventricle, which sends it to the lungs to pick up a fresh supply of oxygen. This oxygen-rich blood returns from the lungs to the left atrium, located at the top left side of the heart, and then it is pumped into the left ventricle. From there it is pumped through vessels called arteries, which deliver oxygen and nutrients to all parts of the body.

6. At the end of the smallest tubes, the air reaches the millions of tiny balloonlike sacs, called alveoli. Each of the alveoli is surrounded by tiny blood vessels, called capillaries. This is where the oxygen-rich blood cells enter the body each time air is inhaled and where carbon dioxide is removed when air is exhaled. (7, 8, 9)

7. Answers will vary.

8. The epiglottis prevents food or liquid from entering the trachea.

9. The circulatory and respiratory systems work together to deliver oxygen and other important nutrients to all of the cells in our bodies.

10. Platelets are important in order to stop bleeding and allow wounds to heal.

25. Nervous System, p. 76

1. a. F (7), brain
   b. T (4)
   c. T (14, 15)
   d. F (3), spinal cord

2. d (2, 4, 26)
3. d (3, 10, 17)
4. Nerves are bundles of nerve cells, or neurons. Neurons can send signals to and receive signals from other neurons. (5, 6)

5. Many areas have specialized functions. Hypothalamus: controls involuntary body operations, such as heartbeat and blood circulation; cerebral cortex: controls thought and voluntary action; cerebellum: controls body movement; thalamus: sends out feelings of pain, touch, and temperature to other parts of the brain.

6. The central nervous system is related to every system in the body. Answers will vary.

7. Signals travel along neurons in the form of nerve impulses. When an impulse reaches a gap between one neuron and the next, a chemical is released and the impulse can be sent on.

8. A message of pain is sent to the spinal cord that relays it to a nerve traveling to the brain.

9. The nervous system is made up of the brain, spinal cord, and nerves. The brain and spinal cord make up the central nervous system, which receives information from all parts of the body, processes it, and sends instructions to other parts of the body. The nerves that carry information to and from the central nervous system make up the peripheral nervous system.

10. The brain is the body's control center. It sends messages to and receives them from all parts of the body.

26. Digestive System, p. 79

1. a. F (8), chyme

   b. F (14), duodenum

   c. F (17), small intestine

   d. T (19)

2. b

3. a

4.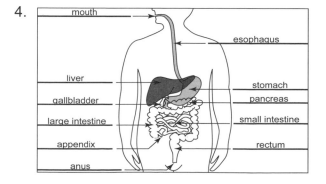

5. Digestion helps change food into smaller nutrients before they are absorbed into the blood and carried to cells throughout the body to provide energy and nutrients to the cells.

6. Your stomach produces gastric juices that help to break down food into chyme. It also helps kill bacteria that might be in the food you ate. Then the liquid food slowly moves into the small intestine. (8, 9, 10)

7. Answers will vary.

8. Answers will vary.

9. Hormones work with the brain to regulate the intake of food for energy. Saliva in the mouth moistens the food and breaks it down. The food passes through the esophagus, and the walls of the esophagus contract to squeeze the food down into the stomach. The stomach produces gastric juices, which break down the food into a liquid mixture called chyme. The liquid food slowly moves into the small intestine, which has three sections: the duodenum, the jejunum, and the ileum. The duodenum receives the partially digested food from the stomach and begins the absorption of nutrients for your body. This is where digestive juices from the liver and pancreas help break down the fats, protein, and starch in the food before it passes to the jejunum. The jejunum is the coiled middle section of the small intestine. The third and final section of the small intestine is the ileum. The inner wall of the small intestine is covered with projections called villi that absorb nutrients into the blood. The nutrient-rich blood is then carried to your liver for more processing before it is carried around the body. Water and any food that cannot be digested move into the large intestine, called the colon. There, any remaining water and some minerals are absorbed into your bloodstream. After most of the nutrients are removed from the food mixture, there is waste left over that your body can't use. This waste matter, called feces, then passes into the second part of the large intestine, called the rectum, where it remains until you are ready to go to the bathroom.

10. Answers will vary.

27. Reproductive System, p. 82

1. a. T (8)

    b. T (16)

    c. F (11), zygote

    d. T (23)

2. d (4)

3. b

4. mitosis: the process of cell division for the different types of body cells such as bone cells, blood cells, and skin cells
    meiosis: how sex cells form; the nucleus of a sex cell divides twice, making four new cells that each have half the number of original chromosomes

5. It is important so that living organisms can produce more of their own kind. (1)

6. The female will lay her eggs, and then the male will later spray his sperm over the eggs to fertilize them. (9)

7. Because it is determined by the availability of food, water, and adequate shelter.

8. All living things go through cycles. Cells go through the cell cycle, living things go through the reproductive cycle to reproduce, and all living organisms go through the life cycle.

9. Sometimes true. Human sperm cell and ovum have 23 chromosomes each. When they join, they become one cell with 46 chromosomes. Each cell of the new offspring has the same number of chromosomes as each body cell of the parents.

10. Meiosis makes sexual reproduction possible.

28. Classification of Organisms, p. 85

1. a. T (7)

    b. F (13,14), family

    c. F (22, 23), larger sizes than

    d. T (33)

2. d

3. a

4. b (27)

5. **Animals**: accept any animals

    Plants: accept any plants

    Fungi: mold and mushrooms

    Protists: algae and protozoa

6. eubacteria (36)

7. Mammalia class (or mammals); Characteristics could include: mammary (milk-producing) glands in the female, warm-blooded, vertebrates, and the presence of hair or fur, live birth, and breathe with lungs

8. Fish characteristics could include: breathe with gills, live in water, most have scales, most lay eggs, cold-blooded, and vertebrates

9. Kingdom: Animal; grizzly bear and any other animals can be listed

    Phylum: Chordata; grizzly bear and any vertebrate animals including other mammals, reptiles, amphibians, birds, or fish

    Class: Mammalia (or mammals); grizzly bear and any mammals, such as dogs, horses, elephants, rats, or whales

    Order: Carnivora; grizzly bears and other mammals that eat meat, such as lions, polar bears, or dogs

    Family: Ursidae; grizzly, panda, brown, black, and polar bears

    Genus: Ursus; grizzly, brown, black, and polar bear

    Species: Ursus Arctos; grizzly and all brown bears

    Sub-species: Horribilis; grizzly bear

10. The two main two groups that plants are divided into are vascular and nonvascular. Nonvascular plants are not divided any further and include plants such as mosses. Vascular plants are separated into two groups: seedless and seed. Seedless plants include plants such as ferns and horsetails. Seed plants include all plants that produce flowers and other seed casings, such as cones. The seed group is separated by whether or not the plants produce flowers. Gymnosperm plants do

not produce flowers but do produce cones and include plants such as pine trees. Angiosperm plants produce flowers and include a wide variety of plants, such as orange trees and all other flowering plants.

29. Function of Plant Parts, p. 88

1. a. F (8) some

   b. F (14, 18) sunny days

   c. F (D) inner or middle

   d. T (14, 15)

2. c (16, 17)

3. d

4. cuticle and epidermis

5. Chlorophyll is the green pigment that makes the leaf green. (19)

6. Table:

Plant Part	Job Description
leaf	make food for plant / photosynthesis
stem	support the plant
root	hold plant in place and absorb water and minerals from soil
xylem	transport water and minerals
phloem	carry glucose

7. **Photosynthesis:** water+carbon dioxide+sunlight→oxygen+glucose (or sugar)

   Cellular Respiration: glucose+oxygen→water+carbon dioxide+energy

8. Some inferences could be: the cuticle is transparent, protects the leaf, is very thin, and allows water and air to pass through it.

9. Some problems could be: not enough sunlight; not enough air (carbon dioxide); not enough water; or through transpiration, the plant may lose too much water.

30. Reproduction in Plants, p. 91

1. a. F (3), only one parent

   b. T (8)

   c. F (7), ovule

   d. F (14), is fertilized

2. c

3. d

4. pollination and dissemination (8 or 9 and 23, 24, or 26)

5. The petals drop off of the flower. The ovary develops into fruit. The fruit grows, and the sepal withers away. The seeds have developed in the center of the fruit.

6. Each box below shows possible answers. The student should have at least one answer per box.

Dissemination	
raccoon	carry hitchhiker seed on fur or eat fruit with seeds
bear	carry hitchhiker seed on fur or eat fruit with seeds
wind	blows seed to new place
water	carries seed to new place

7. Some possible answers are: warm weather, rain, good soil conditions, and fresh air

8. nectar, pollen, anther (9)

9. **Compare:** both produce pollen; both can spread pollen by wind; both use pollen to fertilize ovule

   Contrast: angiosperm plants can use pollinators to transfer pollen and produce seeds in a flower, which can contain both the male and female cells and, therefore, can self-pollinate; gymnosperm plants produce seeds in cones and each cone is either male or female.

10. Possible recommendation:

   The plants are probably not getting pollinated. The plants could be planted outside where nature would help with the pollination. Macey could also open her window and screen for a while each day in hopes that insects would help with pollination. If the plants are not pollinated, then the plant cannot be fertilized to produce fruit. (Accept other pollination answers that make sense.)

31. Invertebrates, p. 94

1. a. F (D), large
   b. T (4)
   c. F (D), the ocean
   d. T (10)
2. d
3. d (13, 17)
4. 19.2%
5. egg, nymph, adult
6. egg, larva, pupa, adult
7. The pupa cannot eat because it is sealed inside a cocoon and has no way to obtain food.
8. **Head**: pair of antennae, eyes, and mouth
   Thorax: six legs and wings
   Abdomen: body systems
9. Two insects, arachnids such as spiders and scorpions, crustaceans such as lobsters and/or other arthropods can be named. Details could include: exoskeleton, three body section and metamorphosis for insects, and segmented or jointed body.
10. Using the chart from the lesson, check to see if the answer includes one of the animals and the characteristics from each of the phyla: arthropods, echinoderms, cnidarians, and mollusks.

32. Vertebrates, p. 97

1. a. T (5)
   b. F (30), stays similar to its surroundings
   c. T (16)
   d. F (D), after
2. d
3. b
4. The mammary glands produce milk to nourish mammal's young. (10)
5. Bunting and Northern Cardinal: thick beaks are strong enough to crack seeds.
6. American Robin: its long, thin beak is used to poke deep into soil.
7. Three characteristics should be in each section:

   Mammals: mammary glands, birth live young, hair or fur

   Birds: young hatch from eggs, wings, feathers, beaks, most fly

   Both: vertebrate, endoskeleton, warm-blooded, care for young, limbs
8. At least twelve characteristics should be listed:

   Reptiles: dry skin
   Amphibians: smooth, moist skin

   Fish: fins; live in water only

   Reptile and amphibians: live on land and in water; breathe with lungs

   Reptiles and fish: scales

   Amphibians and fish: live in water; gills

   All three: cold-blooded; vertebrate; endoskeleton; limbs; lay eggs
9. Amphibians such as frogs need to adapt the way they breathe through their lives because they live in the water and on land. The eggs hatch in the water. Thus, the tadpoles live in the water and breathe with gills. As they grow and develop legs, they also develop lungs as a frog. They eventually live on land and breathe with lungs.

33. Earth's Biomes, p. 100

1. a. F (23), are many
   b. T (9)
   c. F (31, 32), a large variety of trees (or many trees)
   d. F (21), much higher than
2. a
3. d
4. They are nocturnal – they rest during the day and are active at night. (26)
5. boreal forest, grassland, and tundra
6. The average temperature ranges from about 8-20 degrees Celsius. The annual precipitation ranges from approx. 20-100 cm.
7. a. Located near the equator, mainly in South America, Africa, and the islands south of continental Asia
   b. Being near the equator causes the rain forests to remain hot all year round.
8. The tundra should be labeled to the far north of North America and could be labeled on any of the other far north areas.

The temperate forests should be labeled between the Tropic of Cancer and the Arctic Circle and between the Tropic of Capricorn and the Antarctic Circle.

9. Answer may include: poor soil; lacking in nutrients; makes it difficult for plants to grow.

10. A description of the student's biome should be given, along with climate (temperature range and precipitation range). Also included should be a combination of the abiotic factors (water, air, sunlight, and soil) and how they affect the biotic factors (all living things).

34. Ecosystems, p. 103

1. a. F (22), herbivores
   b. F (11), one pond
   c. T (24)
   d. F (22), a herbivore
2. b
3. c
4. Answers will vary. The answer should describe the niche of an animal not mentioned in this lesson. This should include what the animal eats, who eats it, where it lives, and any other details about this animal's role.
5. Producers do not consume other organisms. They make their own food through photosynthesis. (20, 21)
6. Answers will vary but could include any living things, such as a variety of animals and plants, that could live in any forest around the world.
7. A drawing of the sun should be added to the food web diagram. One arrow should be pointing from the sun to the grass and one arrow should be pointing from the sun to the acorns.
8. A diagram of the food chain should begin with the sun, and then an arrow should point from the sun to a producer (any plant is fine). From there, an arrow should point to a primary consumer (any herbivore or omnivore is fine; a cow is one example). From there, an arrow should point to a human. (Additional consumers may be included, but the arrow should only follow one path.)

9. A food web should be drawn. It should include the same links from the food chain in #8. Additional producers and consumers should also be added to diagram the variety of food that animals consume.

10. The aquarium ecosystem may describe a freshwater, saltwater, or other ecosystem that has biotic and abiotic items small enough to place in an aquarium. A description of two niches should be included.

35. Plate Tectonics: Mountains, Volcanoes, and Earthquakes, p. 107

1. a. T (1)
   b. F (13), mantle
   c. T (20)
   d. F (24), convergent boundaries
2. b (19)
3. c (29)
4. Places where plates move apart are called divergent boundaries. At convergent boundaries, the plates are actually moving toward each other, causing a collision. A transform fault boundary occurs when plates slide past each other in different directions without moving up or down. (19, 21, 29)
5. Earth's continents fit together at one time as one gigantic continent called Pangaea. (8, 9)
6. An earthquake is the rigorous shaking of Earth due to sudden plate movements. Heat from deep in Earth's interior causes the rock in the mantle to become hotter and rise upward. Then it squeezes between the edges of two plates, or plate boundaries, which forces the plates apart. (31)
7.-8. Richter scale: rates the magnitude of earthquakes from 1 to 10. The rating stays the same.
Mercalli scale: measures the effects or damage of an earthquake. It may change depending on the location of the measurements and how far the location is from the epicenter.
9. The farther away from the epicenter a place is, the lower the effects of the earthquake will be. It may also depend on whether the location is densely populated or not.
10. Volcanoes are formed at convergent plate boundaries as hot rock material becomes magma and erupts.

36. Rock Cycle, Erosion, and Deposition, p. 110

1. a. F (7), weathering
   b. T (10)
   c. F (18), extrusive rocks
   d. T (4)
2. c (9)
3. b (28)
4. Igneous rocks form when rock minerals are melted, cooled, and become solid again. (13)
5. Sedimentary rocks are formed from eroded layers of sediment materials, such as deceased plants and animals and pieces of rocks, that settle in layers on top of each other and harden over time. Conglomerates are sedimentary rocks that are made up of pebbles, boulders, or shells that become hardened together in clumps. (20, 23)
6. Metamorphic rock could have once been igneous, sedimentary, or even metamorphic rock that changed through extreme heat and pressure. Metamorphic rocks usually form deep below Earth's surface. Once a metamorphic rock forms, it does not melt; its structure and texture change instead. (24, 26, 27)
7. superposition and original horizontality
8. 10; Scientists use half-life to compare the amount of the original element to the amount of the decay product.
9. Most scientists believe fossils can tell us what type of organisms lived in the past and what their environment was like, which also helps scientists to tell the age of a rock.
10. Once a metamorphic rock forms, it doesn't melt; its structure and texture change instead. Igneous rocks form when rock minerals are melted, cooled, and become solid again.

37. Properties of Rocks and Minerals, p. 113

1. a. T (6);
   b. F (15), hardness;
   c. F (27), opaque;
   d. F (38), density
2. a
3. d
4. Answers will vary but should include: color, hardness, streak, transparency, luster, cleavage, specific gravity, and crystal form or structure. (4)
5. The Mohs' Hardness Scale identifies hardness in rocks and ranks ten minerals from softest to hardest. The number one represents the softest mineral, and number ten represents the hardest. (15, 19, 20)
6. Answers will vary but may include: granite, malachite, feldspar, mica, hornblende, quartz, or amethyst. (9, 12, 23)
7. Answers will vary but should include using the properties of minerals.
8. Answers will vary.
9. The property of transparency describes how well light passes through a mineral. There are three categories of transparency: transparent, translucent, and opaque. It is possible to see through transparent minerals. Some light can pass through translucent minerals, but you cannot see through them. No light can pass through an opaque mineral.
10. A way to test the hardness is to scratch one mineral with another. A harder mineral will scratch a softer mineral.

38. Geological Time, p. 116

1. a. T (7)
   b. T (11)
   c. F (16), Precambrian Era
   d. F (23), Cenozoic Era
2. b (2)
3. c (17)
4. Most scientists believe Earth began with the Precambrian Era that lasted about four billion years and covers the majority of Earth's history. The earliest known marine fossils are believed to date back to this era. Wormlike creatures called Spriggina lived on the ocean floor at the end of the Precambrian Era.

5. Original horizontality is the idea that many kinds of rocks form flat, horizontal layers. Superposition is the idea that in a sequence of rock layers, the bottom layer is the oldest and the top layer is the youngest. (4,5)

6. The Paleozoic Era began when many-celled organisms quickly reproduced. Fossil records during the Cambrian Period of that era imply that there was a large increase in the number of and variety of creatures on Earth, including assorted fish and animals with shells. Scientists believe that trilobites began to appear during this period. This was also the time when the earliest vertebrates began to appear. (19, 20, 21, 22)

7. Fossils help identify the remains of plants and animals. The earliest known marine fossils are believed to date back to the Precambrian Era; many-celled organisms, such as fish and animals with shells, reproduced during the Paleozoic Era; the Mesozoic Era included the first flowering plants, first birds, dinosaurs, and the first mammals.

8. Fossils can tell the history of life and the environments on Earth.

9. Geological time is a scale of millions of years used by geologists to measure Earth's development. It is broken down into eons, eras, periods, epochs, and ages.

10. Fossil records during the Cambrian Period of the Paleozoic Era imply that there was a large increase in the number of and variety of creatures on Earth, including assorted fish and animals with shells. Scientists believe that trilobites began to appear during this period. This was also the time when the earliest vertebrates (animals with backbones) began to appear.

39. Natural Resources, p. 119

1. a. F (3), nonrenewable resource

   b. T (9)

   c. T (19)

   d. F (26), renewable resource

2. d (1)

3. c (3)

4. Reduce means to cut back on the use of resources. Reuse, or don't throw away, items that can be used over again. Recycle, or use existing products to make other products. Examples will vary but could include: reduce – turning off the lights you aren't using; reuse – putting groceries in plastic bags you already have; recycle – taking aluminum cans to a recycling center instead of throwing them away. (33, 35, 37)

5. Some energy sources, such as solar energy, wind energy, geothermal energy (energy from within Earth), biomass energy (energy from plants), and hydropower (energy from water), are renewable resources. (14)

6. Answers will vary.

7. Sewage; from garbage and chemicals

8. Farmers may plant too many crops without crop rotation, they may spray the soil with chemicals, or they may allow farm animals to overgraze. All of these things may damage our natural resources. (7)

9. Answers will vary.

10. Water can become too polluted for use. Pollution is partially due to chemicals in the air and on the ground that are picked up by precipitation, causing runoffs into our lakes, rivers, and streams. Factories that illegally dump waste into water also contribute to pollution. All of this pollution harms Earth's natural resources.

40. Ocean Exploration, p. 122

1. a. T (1)

   b. T (8)

   c. F (17), Mariana Trench

   d. F (11), satellites

2. d (8, 9, 11)

3. a

4. Submersibles are important because underwater exploration is very difficult and very dangerous. The oceans are extremely large bodies of water that are very dark, deep, and exceptionally cold. Submersibles are also necessary because underwater pressure can exceed 16,000 pounds per square inch. (4, 5, 6)

5. The oceans are extremely large bodies of water that are very dark, deep and exceptionally cold. Another factor that contributes to the difficulty of exploration is that underwater pressure can exceed 16,000 pounds per square inch. (5, 6)

6. mountain ranges, volcanoes, plateaus, trenches, plants, and animals (13, 21)

7. 44.1 psi

8. Sea level is the sunlit zone – home to many plants and animals; twilight zone – some light from the sun, but not enough for plants to grow; deep ocean zone – sunless and very cold; abyssal zone – dark, icy cold bottom layer of the ocean; hadal zone- deepest trenches.

9. Answers will vary.

10. Answers will vary.

41. Ocean Resources, p. 125

1. a. F (5), Biological resources
   b. T (13)
   c. F (21), fresh water
   d. T (25)

2. c

3. d

4. Answers will vary but may include: living organisms provide recreational enjoyment for people who view and study marine life in aquariums. Ocean water is also used as a coolant in power plants or for the actual production of power. Offshore wind farms, turbines that use waves and currents, and ocean thermal energy conversion are just some of the newest technologies being developed to capture some of the oceans' energy. (16, 22, 24)

5. Clam harvesting has declined since 1970 probably because of a limited supply of clams due to over-harvesting and/or pollution.

6. Biological resources: food, chemicals secreted from living organisms, and living organisms; physical resources: sand, salt, gravel, water, and minerals; both: oil and gas

7. Answers will vary but may include limiting the amount of fish caught by commercial fishermen or closing off areas of fishing for limited times and then reopening them.

8. Answers will vary but may include – Sea life: control over-harvesting of shellfish and/or fish; Ocean water: control pollution and water waste; Fossil fuels: conserve energy and use of petroleum products, recycle products.

9. Answers will vary but may include: food, clothing, energy, minerals, travel, shipping, recreation, sand, salt, gravel, water, oil, and gas.

10. Answers will vary but may include toothpaste, water, lunchmeat, clothing, salt, or gas.

42. Earth, Moon, and Sun, p. 128

1. a. F (2), 365 days
   b. F (15), 28 days
   c. T (5)
   d. T (30)

2. b (11)

3. c (4)

4. We only see one side of the moon because it rotates in the same length of time that it takes to revolve around Earth. This is called captured motion. (19, 20)

5. Lunar eclipses happen when the moon passes through Earth's shadow and doesn't get sunlight for a short period of time. Solar eclipses happen when Earth is in the moon's shadow and the sunlight is blocked from Earth for a short time. (30, 31)

6.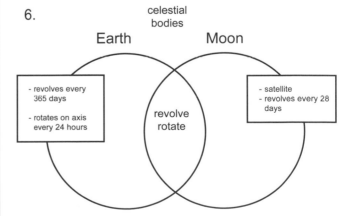

7. The moon is between Earth and the sun. The moon can't be seen because the part the sun is shining on isn't visible from Earth.

8. The moon's shape seems to change shape because what we see from Earth depends on the angle at which the sun's light is hitting the moon.

9. It takes 24 hours (one day) for Earth to rotate on its axis. The axis is an imaginary line that goes through Earth from the North and South poles. The part of Earth facing the sun receives light while the other side is dark, which is what gives us day and night.

10. Answers will vary but may include: there would not be seasons; there would be only one season.

43. Weather: Measurement, Causes, and Changes, p. 131

1. a. T (7)

   b. F (19), low-pressure

   c. F (26), precipitation

   d. F (15), barometers

2. a (11)

3. d (7)

4. Weather is the condition of the atmosphere near Earth's surface. Climate is the weather that characterizes a particular region over a period of time. (5, 33)

5. If a high-pressure system is forecast, then cooler weather and clear skies are coming. A prediction of a low-pressure system will bring warm weather, storms, and rain. (18, 19)

6. The sun's rays have the strongest effect on the middle of Earth (the equator), where the rays hit it directly. (10)

7. Water exists in Earth's atmosphere as water vapor that comes from oceans, rivers, lakes, plants, and many other places. The sun heats the water on Earth and changes it into a gas called water vapor through evaporation. When the air is cooled high up in the atmosphere, the water vapor turns into liquid droplets of water or ice and forms clouds. This process is called condensation. When the cloud droplets or ice crystals become heavy enough, gravity pulls this moisture to Earth as precipitation

in the form of rain, hail, sleet, or snow. This whole process is known as the water cycle.

8. Answers will vary but may include: warns people of high winds, used for sailors, etc.

9. Meteorologists use barometers to measure air pressure, which is created by the atmosphere pressing down on Earth's surface. The amount of pressure air exerts is influenced by the temperature, amount of water vapor, volume, and height of the air above Earth. The amount of humidity in the air is measured using a psychrometer.

10. The sun's rays have the strongest effect on the middle of Earth (the equator) where the rays hit it directly and the ozone layer of the atmosphere is thinner. This warm air then rises and cool air flows in to take its place. This air movement is what causes wind in the atmosphere.

44. Classification of the Sun and Other Stars, p. 134

1. a. F (5), medium-size

   b. F, plasma (6)

   c. T (15)

   d. F (25), brightness

2. c (33)

3. b (25)

4. The brightest stars give off the most energy. The star's size, temperature, and distance from Earth are important factors for how bright a star looks, known as its apparent magnitude. (26, 27)

5. Stars are categorized by their brightness, color, and temperature. (23)

6. About three-quarters of the sun is made of hydrogen and one-quarter is helium. It produces energy through nuclear fusion reactions (a process by which the nuclei of two or more atoms join to form a single, larger nucleus) that turn hydrogen atoms into helium atoms. (9, 10)

7. main sequence stars

8. -5 to -10 absolute magnitude

9. Solar energy is created deep within the core of the sun, where the temperature is 27,000,000 degrees Fahrenheit (15,000,000 degrees Celsius). Heat from the core travels through the radiation and convection zones to the surface of the sun. The next layer of the sun that gives off the light energy that is seen from Earth is called the photosphere. It is the innermost layer of the sun's atmosphere and glows at more than 9,900 degrees Fahrenheit (5,500 degrees Celsius). The atmospheric layer above the photosphere is the chromosphere.

10. Sunspots are small, dark patches that are cooler than surrounding areas in the photosphere layer of the sun.

45. Inner and Outer Solar System, p. 137

1. a. F (2, 3), inner solar system
   b. T (13)
   c. T (15)
   d. T (32)

2. c (9)

3. d (24)

4. The solar system is made up of the sun, the eight official planets, at least three dwarf planets, more than 130 satellites of the planets, comets, asteroids, dust, cosmic rays, and hot plasma. (1)

5. The outer solar system contains Jupiter, Saturn, Uranus, and Neptune. They are sometimes called the Jovian (Jupiterlike) planets or the gas giants because they are mostly made of gas. Some, or maybe all of them, have small, solid cores. (17, 18)

6. The Great Red Spot, located on the surface of Jupiter, is an enormous storm. (21)

7. **Ordering Planet Data**

Closest to Sun to Farthest From Sun	Smallest to Largest	Shortest Year to Longest Year
Mercury	Mercury	Mercury
Venus	Mars	Venus
Earth	Venus	Earth
Mars	Earth	Mars
Jupiter	Neptune	Jupiter
Saturn	Uranus	Saturn
Uranus	Saturn	Uranus
Neptune	Jupiter	Neptune

8. Answers will vary but may include that the longer a planet's year, the farther away it is from the sun.

9. The outer planets include Jupiter, Saturn, Uranus, and Neptune. They are sometimes called the Jovian (Jupiterlike) Planets or the gas giants because they are mostly made of gas, although some, or maybe all of them, may have small, solid cores.
   The inner planets include Mercury, Venus, Earth, and Mars because they are the planets closest to the sun. They are known as terrestrial planets because of their solid, rocky surfaces.

10. Earth is able to support life.